J.G. MONTGOMERY

HAUNTED CASTLES OF ENGLAND

A TOUR OF 99 GHOSTLY FORTRESSES

Llewellyn Worldwide
Woodbury, Minnesota

First Edition
First Printing, 2018

Book design by Bob Gaul
Cover design by Kristi Carlson
Editing by Aaron Lawrence
Interior map illustration by Llewellyn art department

Photos by: Library of Congress, ca 1890–1900 (Arundel, Dover, Hastings, Hurstmonceaux, Pevensey, Rochester, Berkeley, Berry Pomeroy, Corfe, Taunton, Okehampton, Hadleigh, Peveril, Goodrich, Kenilworth, Ludlow, Carlisle, Scarborough, Skipton, Durham); Library of Congress, ca 1902 (Windsor); Library of Congress, ca 1910-1915 (Tattershall); New York Public Library Digital Collection, George Arents Collection (Bodiam, Sudeley, Bolsover, Nottingham, Dudley, Tamworth, Warwick, Lowther, Muncaster, Bolton, Richmond, Ripley, Bamburgh, Barnard, Raby); New York Public Library Digital Collection, Art and Picture Collection (Farnham, St Briavells, Colchester, Kimbolton, Norwich, Naworth); New York Public Library Digital Collection, Art and Picture Collection, a fifteenth century depiction from 1839 (Oxford); New York Public Library, Art and Picture Collection, ca 1787 (Helmsley); New York Public Library, Art and Picture Collection, depiction of before it was destroyed, ca 1839 (Pontefract); New York Public Library, Art and Picture Collection, ca December 28, 1833 (Warkworth)

Llewellyn Publications is a registered trademark of Llewellyn Worldwide Ltd.

Library of Congress Cataloging-in-Publication Data (Pending)
ISBN: 978-0-7387-5778-0

Llewellyn Publications
A Division of Llewellyn Worldwide Ltd.
2143 Wooddale Drive
Woodbury, MN 55125-2989
www.llewellyn.com

Printed in the United States of America

CONTENTS

Three: South West England   75

Four: East England   111

Five: East Midlands   125

Eight: Yorkshire and the Humber   181

Nine: North East England   203

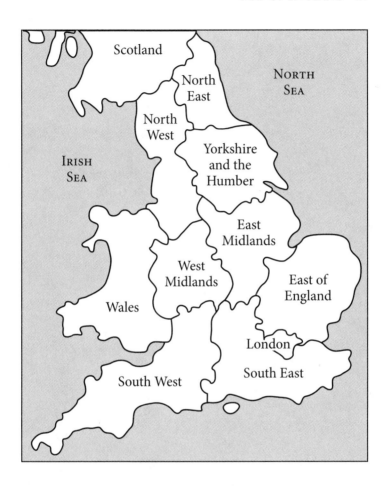

Thanks to Kirsten for her unwavering support and encouragement over the years.

INTRODUCTION

It is a dark, stormy night. You find yourself riding an old mare along a dark, windswept and somewhat unkempt country lane. The wind whistles in the tress and leaves and wisps of thick mist blow across the potholed dirt thoroughfare ahead of you. An owl hoots, spooked by the noise of your horse's tired footsteps, and darts in front of your face. You heart is suddenly racing, and you think you hear something behind you. After all, this is an ancient land, a land of ghosts, pixies, goblins, and all sorts of mythical creatures of the night.

Looking around all you can discern is a deep, foreboding blackness that seems to be following you, as if it is alive and in pursuit. You dig your heels into the old mare and she starts at a canter, whinnying as she does as if she too can feel some sort of evil in this frightening and suggestive atmosphere.

You are new to these parts and have heard the legends and stories and the tales of dark creatures that haunt these woods. But surely these are nothing more than the insane rantings of simple, superstitious country folk. Ghosts and spirits cannot exist, can they? But then again...

The wind suddenly drops and your senses are heightened. Indeed, you can hear your very heart beating in your chest as the old horse continues to canter forward into the night. The mist suddenly becomes thicker, although you don't remember when or where this happened. You glance furtively from side to side but the dark shadows of the woods hide their secrets. You are alone, so alone.

Your breathing is now quicker, and the old horse seems to be labouring. Surely your destination cannot be that far away? You stop and listen intently. Something rustles in the bushes not far from your position and you sit upright, rigid with adrenaline coursing through your veins. You laugh a strangled laugh—an animal, of course. Yes, of course. After all, this is the country. In the distance a lonely bird cries a lament to this most foul of nights.

You goad your horse onward even though she seems to not want to move. And as you do you hear a peculiar but distinct sound behind you in the gloom. You stop and listen intently, but the noise ceases. You permit yourself a quick glance back in the blackness. Now you are imagining things.

You continue on and again you become aware of the noise. It is following you. Stalking you in the night like some foul ghoul or demon escaped from the burning pits of hell. There! What was that?

A small, indistinct shape scurries across the path in front of you, causing the horse to suddenly hesitate. You draw a quick breath and smile. It is nothing more than an animal. You continue your furtive journey, heart pounding, eyes wide open in expectation, nerves jangling like overwrought guitar strings screaming on their limits. You feel a deep, hard lump in the pit of your stomach, a feeling of indescribable dread, of death and misadventure, of loneliness and fear.

But worse, you are sure that you can hear footsteps behind you … ghostly unseen horse hooves that quietly clip-clop on the road behind you and echo in your brain. No, surely it is the wind in the trees or rushing through the bulrushes that line the swampy creek banks that run parallel to the road.

But now there is no wind. Now there is nothing but the darkness. And in that darkness the hooves continue to sound closer and closer, louder and louder. Each step seemingly closer than the last until you believe you can feel the hot breath of a horse breathing down your neck.

And with this you panic, urging your tired old steed onward. You grip the reins in white-knuckled fear and push your body against the saddle as the horse careers forward, now as frightened as you. Ahead of you appears a bridge that leads to a ruined castle, gray and dreary in the dull moonlight. You feel some apprehension at approaching this crumbling relic of the past, but you know that you have no choice as whatever it is that is behind you is infinitely more frightening, infinitely more evil. And it is getting closer. You gulp and cross the bridge riding onward until you reach the overpowering gray bulk that is the castle. You are safe for now...

Everyone, it would seem, even hardened sceptics and disbelievers, has a ghost story. For some reason, in the back of their minds, ghosts may be real. Everyone has known the feeling of their heart racing for a second when they see a shadow moving in the corner of their eye or they feel some sort of presence standing over them as they try to sleep. Or worse still, a tortured face in a window that paralyses their body and retards their breathing to the point that they can hear the blood pumping around their own body.

We can dismiss the supernatural as simply an overactive imagination, a trick of the eye, a lucid waking dream, or a simple illusion or misinterpretation of the facts. We can tell ourselves that the scraping sound at the window is simply a branch being blown in the breeze and that the footsteps heard in the hallway are old timbers creaking and groaning with a change in the air or weather. We are sure that the scratching in the wall is nothing more than mice and that rasping sound you hear sometimes from your bed late at night is nothing more than a bird, perhaps an owl, outside your window.

This is where suggestion takes over, and the imagination, if allowed, runs wild. Indeed, it is a very childlike feeling lying under the covers, eyes straining to see in the darkness that surrounds you, ears tingling at the slightest sound, your body frozen and your breathing almost non-existent. You see, in this environment, ghosts are very real and frightening.

Science has tried in vain to explain ghosts and hauntings and yet, as much as science tells us that they cannot possibly exist, we still can't quite dismiss the notion from our fertile minds that they *might* just exist. After all, how is it that so many people can report the same phenomena time and time again without ever having met or collaborated their stories? We can explain any ghostly encounter as natural phenomenon, but the doubt still remains; for who of us has not lain quietly in their bed, the blankets pulled up tightly to their chin, their breathing ragged and strained as *something* sounds as if it is in the darkened room with us?

Pliny the Younger, also known as Gaius Plinius Caecilius Secundus, was a lawyer, author, and magistrate in ancient Rome, and wrote hundreds of letters over his life. In one he described how a philosopher named Athenodoros had rented an allegedly haunted house in Athens in roughly 100 CE. In the letter he described a ghost that was a dishevelled, aged spectre, bound at feet and hands and rattled chains. Apparently after digging up the bones and giving them a proper burial the haunting ceased and normality returned.

These days nothing much appears to have changed when it comes to ghostlore. In the current day, almost every ghost we see on film or television is based upon some heart-rending or untimely death of an individual who, unable to move on in death is stuck in some sort of supernatural limbo between life and death and as such, hangs around to haunt the living, sometimes extracting a grisly revenge on those who have wronged them in life, or to raise awareness of their plight such as the circumstances of their death. In essence, programs such as *Supernatural* and *Ghost Whisperer* follow the same script as did Shakespeare in a great deal of his writing. After all, what student can forget Banquo's ghost visiting the horrified Macbeth in the great halls of Dunsinane Castle or Hamlet receiving a ghostly visit from his dead father on the ramparts of his castle.

Popular culture, it would seem, is to blame for the present day stereotypical view of a ghost, which we shall see is if not completely incorrect, at least inaccurate to some extent. In popular ghostlore we are mainly exposed to classic or historical hauntings, that is, traditional or historical reports that have been continually retold over many years and in many cases, hundreds of years or even centuries. An example of this is those stories from the Tower of London. These are the ghosts of history books, tourist guidebooks, tradition and legend. Having said this, it does not mean that they are any less valid than modern reports, as many of them have been investigated numerous times by vast numbers of people over many years.

Of course, even with innumerable first-hand reports and stories of ghosts, there will always be sceptics who snort derisively at those who dare to entertain the thought that ghosts may just be real. And yet, try spending the night alone in one of the most haunted places in the world, say a haunted bedroom in an ancient pub or a darkened cellar in a castle in England, and all the logic and scepticism in the world won't help you when you hear a rasping breath in the darkness only a few feet from where you stand or lie.

And this leads us to the subject of this book—castles of England. Castles have long been regarded as prime settings for ghosts and all things supernatural due to their long and unusually bloody histories. From wars to executions, to suicide and untimely death from injury, plague or disease, castles are, for all their majesty and splendor, tragic places where death stalked the cold lonely corridors with regular monotony. These are the places of the bloodiest history, whether it be battles for ownership, the executions of traitors, or the torture of prisoners in the depths of dank, dark, rat-infested dungeons. Could this be the reason why castles are seen as places where ghosts may reside? Can this explain why almost every fortress in England, whether a pile of rubble or a magnificent edifice to the medieval times, comes attached with its own ghosts, or in most cases, multiple ghosts that haunt the grounds, hallways, and stately rooms? With such a history of violence and tragedy, it is little wonder that these places are regarded as haunted.

England is a land of appealing features seemingly embedded in the sense of a deep-rooted and permanent history that emanates from almost every corner of the land. It is a feeling that its rustic towns and quaint villages, hulking castles and towering cathedrals, have fostered over many centuries to create a comfortable and pleasing landscape that the visitor recalls like a favorite arm chair.

A journey through England is a passage through history. A real history, one that you can live and breathe, one that you can feel and be a part of. You can walk serenely around three-thousand-year-old megaliths that stand silently on ancient Neolithic plains or walk the corridors and battlements of medieval castles just as they were patrolled by armor clad soldiers many centuries ago. Or one can walk the ancient chalk cliffs of the south and gaze at the brilliant blue waters of the English Channel before heading west to the land of King Arthur, piskies, and ancient, half-forgotten legends and folklore.

It is a place that inspires contemplation and wonderment, whether wandering aimlessly through quintessential medieval market places, climbing thousand-year-old earthworks, gazing upon chalk-cut giants, or comfortably settled in the corner of a wooden-framed, stone-floored country pub with a roaring fire and a refreshing pint of lager in hand.

It is a land of living history, of memories as far back as history recalls. It is a place of myth and legend, of ghosts and ghouls, of giants and dwarves, or mermaids and other half-remembered, half-whispered-about creatures.

It is also a place of great medieval buildings, from stately manors to cathedrals, abbeys, and castles. And it is the latter that we are interested in considering the wealth of material available. Indeed, the *Castellarium Anglicanum*, an authoritative index of castles in England and Wales that was published in 1983, lists over 1,500 castle sites in England alone. Many of these castles have now completely disappeared and some are no more than a pile of rubble or earthworks. However, for this book we are looking at structures that are still standing. Indeed, some, such as Arundel Castle, are still in use as family homes, whereas others such as Hever Castle are popular tourist destinations.

It should also be noted that a definitive list of castles in England can never be complete, given that there is never complete agreement in every case as to whether the remains of a building are those of a castle, whether a given place is the site of a castle, or whether a surviving building should be considered to be a castle, especially as many sites of Iron Age hill forts or fortifications earlier than the tenth century have become known as castles.

And so, with all this in mind, let us now begin upon a journey of exploration, a journey into the essence of England itself, and visit the castle ghosts of Albion.

ONE

GREATER LONDON

THE TOWER OF LONDON

....

www.hrp.org.uk/tower-of-london/

No ghost book would be complete without at least a reference to the Tower of London, given that it is reputedly the most haunted building in England, if not the entire world. Standing high and menacingly over the iconic Thames River in the London Borough of Tower Hamlets, it was originally commissioned by William the Conqueror in 1078 and completed some nineteen years later. And it has, without doubt, one of the bloodiest histories known to any building in the world.

As such the Tower is the perfect place to start our quest for haunted castles in England. It was one cool, overcast and slightly drizzly day that my partner Kirsten and I visited this amazing set of medieval buildings. As we walked along the

Thames, the Tower seemed to loom out from the gray skies and the river itself seemed angry and gray with a strong tidal flow creating waves that lapped loudly against the ancient stone banks and moored boats. The streets themselves were wet and slippery, and in this sort of atmosphere in this city one could believe in the myriad of ghost stories that have been generated over countless years of human habitation.

Wandering by Traitor's Gate, we notice that the gate itself is old and worn with rusted hinges and fittings and sits ominously in the grayish-green waters of the river. Surrounding this, the stone walls are ancient and worn and at lower levels covered in moss and river slime. The tide at this point of time is low, so we can see the full extent of what gave the castle its grisly name and reputation over the past four hundred or so years—the number of prisoners accused of treason who passed through it on their way to imprisonment, torment and probable death in the Tower itself.

The Tower of London is actually a complex of multiple medieval buildings from different eras set within large stone walls built to keep intruders out. It has played a major role in the history of England, so much so that it is synonymous with the city and has been, over the years, a treasury, a public records office, an armory, home of the Royal Mint, as well as the home of the crown jewels.

A number of extensions were made during the twelfth and thirteenth centuries, and although there have been many modifications and additions to the tower, the original layout essentially remains the same as it was when built. Indeed, in the twelfth century it was fortified by Richard the Lionheart by the addition of an outer wall and a moat. In the following century, Edward I then built an outer wall which completely enclosed the inner wall, as well as filled in the old moat and built a new one, now still plainly visible, except with lush, well-manicured lawns rather than water. Edward used the newly fortified tower as an armory and prison, a place of executions and torture.

Although seemingly impregnable, the Tower has been besieged on numerous occasions as rulers rightly or wrongly believed that the Tower must be controlled in order to control the country. During the fifteenth century, it was used as a prison although it was used in this fashion more so in the sixteenth and seventeenth centuries. Indeed, Elizabeth I was one of the many prominent historical figures who were held captive in the Tower.

Interestingly, although there exists an all-pervading belief that the Tower was a place of death and torture, only a total of seven people were executed within the actual Tower, an insignificant number when compared to other places. Having said this, the executions were commonly held on the Tower Hill and over a period of roughly four hundred years. Over a hundred executions took place, including Simon Sudbury, Archbishop of Canterbury, who was beheaded by an angry mob in 1381; Sir Thomas More, lord chancellor; George Boleyn, brother of Anne Boleyn; and Thomas Howard, 4th Duke of Norfolk.

Before his execution, More requested that his foster daughter be given his headless corpse to bury, and as such he was buried in an unmarked grave in the chapel of St. Peter ad Vincula in the Tower of London. His head, as was the custom for traitors, was fixed upon a pike over London Bridge for a month and would have been thrown into the river if his daughter Margaret Roper had not bribed a nightwatchman and rescued it. His skull is now believed to lie in the Roper Vault of St. Dunstan's Church in Canterbury, though it has also been claimed that it might be within a tomb in Chelsea Old Church. Surprisingly his ghost does not appear to haunt the place of his execution, although it has been reported at Baynards Park in Surrey, even though the majority of the Tudor building was destroyed by fire in 1979.

From initial views, the Tower sits ominously over the River Thames, its four distinctive turrets jutting proudly into the gray skies, designed to strike fear into the residents of medieval London. Often called the White Tower, for obvious reasons, its primary function was as a royal palace, but over time it became a prison for high status or royal prisoners with many executions being held on the green outside the Tower, including William of Hastings in 1483, Anne Boleyn in 1536, and Lady Jane Grey in 1554. The Tower was also used as a prison during the two world wars, and twelve men were executed for espionage, with the last person to be executed being a German spy by the name of Josef Jakobs in 1941. Not surprisingly, the Tower of London was badly damaged by German bombers during the Second World War, later to be repaired and opened to the public. Today it is protected as a World Heritage Site and attracts over two million visitors each year.

The seemingly most persistent of all ghosts in the Tower is that of Anne Boleyn, who was married to King Henry VIII before being executed in May of 1536. Numerous sightings of her ghost have been reported most often close to the site where she was executed. Her headless body has been seen wandering the Tower's lonely corridors and has also been seen leading a procession down the aisle of a chapel. Apparently in 1882 a Captain of the Guard saw a light burning in the locked Chapel Royal, and when he went to investigate, witnessed a figure who he believed was Anne leading a stately procession of knights and ladies in medieval-style clothing. Strangely, although she appeared to have a head in this case, her face was averted. The procession then disappeared from view, leaving the witness shaken and puzzled.

In another famous and equally perplexing case, a guard saw a figure in a brown velvet gown emerge from the mist and move slowly toward him. Surprised, he challenged the figure several times and, receiving no reply, advanced upon the figure with bayonet fixed. As he drew closer he noticed that the figure's bonnet appeared completely empty and that it had no face. Panicking, the guard stabbed at it with the bayonet, only for it to go straight through the figure. Later that morning, his superiors found him unconscious and accused him of sleeping on duty. However, other guards came to the man's aid stating that they too had seen the mysterious lady. They concluded that it must have been the ghost of Anne Boleyn, given the lack of a face or head.

Apart from Anne Boleyn, who seems to appear quite regularly, and Sir Walter Raleigh, who was beheaded in the Old Palace Yard at the Palace of Westminster on October 29, 1618, the Tower has an excess of ghostly occupants ranging from Thomas Becket and Catherine Howard—whose ghost has been seen running down the hallway screaming for help. Other strange sightings include funeral carriages and an unknown woman with a veil but no face.

At one time the Tower was the home to the Royal menagerie, which included lions, birds, monkeys, an elephant, bears, and, in one bizarre report from 1815, a ghostly bear. Lunging at it with a bayonet, the sentry found the weapon going straight through thin air.

Other ghosts of the Tower include those of Thomas Becket, Henry VI, and Guy Fawkes. Indeed, the ghost of Sir Walter Raleigh is said to wander around the Tower grounds just as he did when he was imprisoned there. In 1983, a Yeoman Guard on duty in the Bloody Tower reported seeing his ghost and a year or so later he was again seen in the same area by a different guard. And like George Jeffreys "the Hanging Judge," Raleigh seems to appear in multiple places. Likewise, Thomas Becket, who was murdered in 1170 at Canterbury Cathedral, also appears at the Tower at the place of his death.

Lady Arbella Stuart is one of the Tower's most famous ghosts. A noblewoman who was at one time considered a possible successor to Queen Elizabeth I of England, it is said that her ghost haunts the Queen's House on Tower Green. A direct descendant of Henry VII, she was the only child of Charles Stuart, 1st Earl of Lennox and, according to records, married the nephew of Lady Jane Grey, William Seymour. However, the marriage was seen as a threat because it did not have the permission of King James I. As a result, Arbella was put under house arrest in Lambeth and her husband sent to the Tower. Arbella plotted to get William and escape to France, but William missed the rendezvous and Arbella sailed alone. Tragically, she was recognized and was sent back to England and imprisonment in the Tower.

In her final days as a prisoner in the Tower of London, Arbella refused to eat and soon fell ill before dying on September 25, 1615, although many believe that she was in fact murdered. She was buried in Westminster Abbey. Ironically, her husband William managed to flee England to France.

The Queen's House on Tower Green, home of the Resident Governor and his family, is said to be the most haunted building in the entire Tower complex and has been the site of a number of strange and disturbing events. Indeed, Major

General Geoffrey Field, who was Resident Governor of the Tower from 1994 to 2006, once stated:

> Soon after we arrived in 1994, my wife Janice was making up the bed in the Lennox room when she felt a violent push in her back which propelled her right out of the room! No one had warned us that the house was haunted—but we then discovered that every resident has experienced something strange in that room! The story goes that the ghost is that of Arbella Stuart, a cousin of James I, who was imprisoned and then possibly murdered in that room. Several women who slept there since have reported waking in terror in the middle of the night feeling they were being strangled, so just in case we made it a house rule not to give unaccompanied women guests the Lennox room.

Lady Jane Grey, who ruled England for just nine days before being executed in 1554 for refusing to recant her religion, is also believed to haunt the long, gloomy halls and corridors of this ancient building. Her ghost was last seen by two guardsmen in 1957 on the anniversary of her death. The ghost of her husband, Lord Guildford Dudley, who was also executed, has been seen in another tower, apparently weeping for his lost love.

The Tower was also the scene of the strange disappearance and probable murder of the young princes Edward V and Richard Duke of York in 1483. Edward was 12 years of age at the time and Richard only 10. Legend has it that sometime after their deaths, guards witnessed the ghostly figures of two small boys on some stairs in the Tower. However, the fate of the two boys remained unknown until 1674 when some workmen found a hidden chest containing two small skeletons, presumably those of the missing boys. They were subsequently given a royal burial.

And yet as disturbing as this may be, one of the grisliest of all ghostly apparitions in the Tower would have to be that of the seventy-year-old Countess of Salisbury, last of the Plantagenets, who was executed in 1541. When she was taken for execution she refused to put her head on the block and tried to escape by running away, forcing the executioner to run after her and hack her to death. Her ghost has been seen recreating this gruesome scene, and some have reported seeing the shadow of an executioner's axe chopping down at the scene of her execution.

There is also the White Lady of the massive White Tower, one of the oldest and most foreboding buildings in the complex. She is said to have stood once at a window waving to little children at the building on the opposite side, and her perfume impregnates the air at the entrance to St. John's Chapel.

Also in the White Tower, guards have reported a horrible crushing sensation upon entering the place where King Henry VIII's impressive suits of armor are exhibited. A guard who was patrolling the grounds one night reported the sensation of someone throwing a cloak over him. When he tried to free himself, the cloth was seized from behind and pulled tightly around his throat by his unseen attacker.

Humorously, it was also once reported that a guard who stopped to rest as he made his nightly rounds once had an unnerving encounter. After he had sat on a window ledge and removed his shoe, he began rubbing his foot when a voice behind him whispered, "There's only you and I here." The guard responded, "Just let me get this bloody shoe on and there'll only be you!"

The Tower complex is a wonder, ghosts or no ghosts, as it contains a wealth of treasures from weaponry to armor to the Crown Jewels. Indeed, a visit to London would not be complete without a tour of the grounds and Tower itself where one can admire the iconic Beefeaters or walk along these ancient battlements knowing that, at some stage in history, a king, queen, or royal dignitary once walked on the very same stone. And who knows, according to some, they still do.

BRUCE CASTLE

....

www.haringey.gov.uk/bruce-castle-museum

Bruce Castle, formerly known as the Lordship House, is a sixteenth-century manor house that is one of the oldest surviving brick houses in England. The house is named after the House of Bruce, who previously owned the land. Sir William Compton, who was the Groom of the Stool to Henry VIII, purchased the manor in 1514, but there's no solid proof he ever lived in the home. The earliest known reference of the building was made in 1516, when Henry VIII met his sister Margaret, Queen of Scots, at "Maister Compton's House behind Tottenham."

Bruce Castle is currently a museum and stores the historical archives of Haringey, a borough of London. It also features a permanent exhibition of the past, present, and future of the borough that includes photography, a focus on Rowland Hill, postal history, and historical documents. It also holds, according to some, a ghostly lady, that of Constantia, daughter of Sir Richard Lucy, 1st Baronet of Broxbourne, and Elizabeth Cock and who is said to have committed suicide in 1680.

The earliest recorded reference to her ghost appeared in 1858 in the *Tottenham & Edmonton Advertiser* and read as follows: "A lady of our acquaintance was introduced at a party to an Indian Officer who, hearing that she came from Tottenham, eagerly asked if she had seen the Ghostly Lady of Bruce Castle. Some years before he had been told the following story by a brother officer when encamped on a march in India. One of the Lords Coleraine had married a beautiful lady and while she was yet in her youth had been seized with a violent hatred against her—whether from jealousy or not is not known. He first confined her to the upper part of the house and subsequently still more closely to the little rooms of the clock turret. These rooms looked out on the balconies: the lady one night succeeded in forcing her way out and flung herself with child in arms from the parapet. The wild despairing shriek aroused the household only to find her and her infant in death's clutches below. Every year as the fearful night comes round (it is in November) the wild form can be seen as she stood on the fatal parapet, and her despairing cry is heard floating away on the autumnal blast."

Although there have been few sightings in recent times, she is not the only ghostly visitation to appear at this ancient country house as, according to Andrew Green in his book *Our Haunted Kingdom*, a couple reported to him that, while walking on the grounds of the castle they encountered "a large number of people in eighteenth-century costume, apparently enjoying a festive occasion." Oddly enough, it was also noted that, "despite the couple of dozen people present and the obvious frivolity, there was no sound and the figures seemed to glide rather than walk."

It was also reported that a few days later a couple spent the night in the place and reported seeing "a dozen apparitions, all in olden-days dress… when approached… the crowd just melted into the walls."

HAMPTON COURT PALACE

···················

www.hrp.org.uk/hampton-court-palace

Hampton Court Palace, although technically not a castle, is a royal palace in the borough of Richmond. In 1494, Courtier Giles Daubeney took out a lease on the property, as he needed a house close to London. Little is known about Daubeney's Hampton Court, except that he played host to Henry VII on a number of occasions as it was a peaceful retreat away from the hustle and bustle of the burgeoning city. Daubeney died in 1508 and the site was taken over by Thomas Wolsey, soon to become a Cardinal as well as Lord Chancellor of England. Apart from that he was also a close friend of Henry VIII and held a number of other influential posts.

Wolsey, a man of great ambition, soon set about refurbishing the house, turning it into a magnificent palace, adding new extravagant private chambers for his own use, as well as three suites for the new royal family, one each for King Henry VIII, Queen Katherine of Aragon, and their daughter Princess Mary.

Although Wolsey was criticized by many of his peers for his extravagant lifestyle, this is not what brought about his fall from grace. Indeed, by the late 1520s, Henry was desperate to obtain a divorce from his first wife, lusting after the much younger Anne Boleyn. However, after years of political manoeuvring and discussions, the Pope didn't grant the divorce, which rapidly led to a falling out between Henry and Wolsey, with the latter losing both Hampton Court and his other residence, York Place, to the King in 1529.

Henry VIII, having seized the palace for himself, began an extravagant and expensive refurbishment program including tennis courts, bowling alleys, lavish gardens, kitchens, a new chapel, an enormous communal dining hall, and a hunting park.

Following Henry's death in 1547, Hampton Court was again used as a country retreat away from the business and politics of central London. However, the place remained largely as it had been until the following century when William of Orange (William III) began another massive rebuilding and expansion project, which destroyed much of the old Tudor palace.

Originally intended to rival Versailles, work ceased in 1694, leaving the palace with two distinct contrasting architectural styles—Tudor and Baroque, which is pretty much how it stands to the present day. King George II was the last monarch to reside in the palace.

Catherine Howard is probably the most famous of the palace's many ghosts. She has been reported in the palace's Haunted Gallery on a number of occasions and some have even claimed to have photographed her shadowy figure. She was accused of adultery by Henry VIII and, as the story goes, after she heard that Henry was told of her supposed infidelity, she ran down the corridors to the Chapel in order to plead for her life. However, the guards quickly intercepted her, and dragged her screaming back to her rooms. Later she was taken to the Tower of London and executed.

Interestingly, guests and staff at the palace have reported hearing Catherine's scream from the gallery and on one evening in 1999, during different tours of the palace, two female visitors fainted in exactly the same spot in the same gallery where the screams of Catherine have been heard.

According to Ernest Law in *A Short History of Hampton Court* (1897), on one occasion a female form dressed in white was noticed floating down the Haunted Gallery "towards the door of the Royal Pew, and just as she reaches it, has been observed to hurry back with disordered garments and a ghastly look of despair, uttering at the same time the most unearthly shrieks, till she passes through the door at the end of the gallery".

Ian Franklin, a first aider at the palace has stated, "When I hear over the radio that a visitor has fainted, I always head straight to the Haunted Gallery, even before I'm told the location of the incident. More often than not, that's where it happens."

The Grey Lady of Hampton Court is another of the palace's many ghosts. Sybil Penn, a nurse and servant to Prince Edward, later became a lady-in-waiting to Edward's older sister and successor Queen Elizabeth I, and she looked after the Queen when she fell ill from smallpox in 1562. Her devotion to the Queen ultimately led to her death from the same disease, and she was buried at the church of St Mary's in the village of Hampton near the palace.

The first reports of her ghost began in 1829 when St Mary's Church was demolished for rebuilding and her tomb was disturbed. Soon after, people began to report strange noises throughout the court including the constant whirring of a spinning wheel attributed to Sybil. Sightings of her have been reported in various Tudor cloisters and courtyards.

Indeed, in 2015, twelve-year-old Holly Hampsheir, was amazed and somewhat shaken to find a strange anomaly on a photograph she took of her cousin Brook McGee at the palace. McGee later stated that, "I was totally freaked out. I didn't see anything. People say the room goes cold when ghosts appear but we had no idea. We haven't slept properly since."

Holly's mother Angie added, "I was speechless. There was no one else in that room and she's floating through the rope. Those ropes were alarmed."

And yet, for all its eeriness, this picture is not the most compelling piece of photographic evidence to emerge from the palace as, in October 2003, a ghostly figure was captured on CCTV while security staff reviewed CCTV footage.

After investigating and securing some open doors, security staff returned to inspect the CCTV footage. On the first occasion, the doors flew open without any sign of anyone opening them. However, on the second occasion, the very next day, the staff were shocked to see a figure, in what appeared to be period dress, appear and then close the doors. This pattern was repeated on the third day, however, like the first occurrence, minus the ghostly figure.

Oddly enough, it was not just the security staff who reported seeing something strange. A visitor wrote in the palace's visitor book that she thought she had also seen the apparition of a large man near the same doors.

A member of the security team, Luke Wiltshire, recalled an occasion when he was called out at 3:00 a.m. to accompany an engineer to check a fire alarm in Fountain Court. They both heard the sound of footsteps running away up a flight of stairs although it was impossible for anyone to have been there.

Manuela Pessina, one of the Royal Palace's senior guides also noted, "we get a lot of sightings and unexplained phenomena and it's a very, very spooky place, especially at night. To be honest though, everywhere in Hampton Court gives you chills when you are working late. It's not uncommon for staff to report a feeling of being watched or having doors inexplicably slam behind them when there's no one around."

Apart from this, people have reported a ghostly monk who stalks Henry VIII's apartments. Staff and guests have sighted a large hooded figure with a deformed face lurking in doorways. In the lavish gardens is the Long Water, an artificial lake that runs eastward from the back of the palace. Apparently in 1887 a three-year-old boy ran off and drowned in the lake, a tragedy that would also befall a young girl in 1927 after she had gone to feed the ducks. Forty years later, a four-year-old boy narrowly avoided the same fate, luckily being rescued by a passerby. When asked by his mother why he had leapt into the icy waters, he reportedly replied, "To play with the other children."

TWO

SOUTH EAST ENGLAND

AMBERLEY CASTLE

West Sussex

....

www.amberleycastle.co.uk

Originally constructed as a twelfth-century manor house and fortified in 1377, Amberley Castle was used as a fortress by the bishops of Chichester and now operates as a hotel. During the English Civil War, it was a Royalist stronghold, and Oliver Cromwell ordered General William Waller to attack the castle, resulting in the loss of twenty feet from the height of the walls and the destruction of the Great Hall.

The castle was later sold but once again given back to the Bishop of Chichester after the Restoration of the Monarchy in 1660.

In 1872, the castle was sold to Lord Zouche, who used it as a hunting lodge before selling it to Henry Fitzalan-Howard, fifteenth Duke of Norfolk in 1893, after which it was extensively modernized. Since then it has passed through a number of hands.

The castle has its own resident ghost, named Emily. Who she was is unknown, but her apparition is easily the most commonly encountered spirit. It is believed that she committed suicide, however, her reasons for doing so are unknown.

She has been described as having long brown hair and wearing a Victorian-style dress, and has been seen walking along corridors and even through walls. She is known to be a friendly spirit and those who have encountered her remark that they feel a strange calmness in her presence.

Another resident spirit, however, does not seem so friendly, indeed, though no one has actually seen him, many people passing through a certain room in the castle have claimed to have suddenly felt an intense feeling of having someone right behind them, as well as being watched. Fortunately, this spirit seems to be restricted to the one room that is directly above the portcullis.

ARUNDEL CASTLE
West Sussex

....

www.arundelcastle.org

Arundel Castle is a restored medieval castle that was first owned by Roger de Montgomery in 1067. Roger, who was either a cousin or half-brother of William the Conqueror, was rewarded for his loyalty and was granted land in the Welsh Marches and across the country. The original structure was a motte-and-double-bailey castle.

The castle has been under the ownership of the family of the Duke of Norfolk for over four hundred years, and it is the principal seat of the Norfolk family. Grade I, it was damaged during the English Civil War and then restored in the eighteenth and nineteenth centuries. Today the castle remains the principal seat of the Dukes of Norfolk and most of the castle and its grounds are open to the public.

It is a stunning and wondrous sight sitting in forty acres of grounds and containing priceless works of art, ranging from paintings and furniture, tapestries and stained glass, to sculptures and carving, as well as heraldry and armor. In the light of a warm summer day, it does not appear haunted in any way. However, this is not the case.

A ghost known as the Blue Man and suspected to be from the period of Charles II is said to browse books in the library while the ghost of a young boy who is thought to have worked in the kitchens two hundred years ago and who was beaten frequently by his master, appears scrubbing pots and pans and scurrying around the kitchen. There have also been reports of people hearing the banging and crashing of kitchen utensils even though the area is uninhabited.

The ghost of a young woman dressed in white has also been seen on moonlit nights wandering around Hiorne's

Tower, located behind the castle in Arundel Park and designed in the eighteenth century by architect Francis Hiorne. It is thought that she committed suicide, throwing herself off the Tower after losing the love of her betrothed.

As well, a ghostly white bird has been seen fluttering around the windows of the castle and its appearance is said to coincide with the sudden death of a resident of the castle. Interestingly, various Dukes used to keep white American Owls at the castle in the past.

In 1958, another strange sighting was made by a footman who was working late one night on the ground floor. Apparently he was walking near the servant's quarters and saw what he thought to be a man walking in front of him. As he got closer to the apparition it faded and disappeared.

My visit to the castle in 2010, however, was uneventful—its ghosts deciding to remain quiet and hidden from view. And yet, wandering its ancient corridors with carved arches and cracked stone floors one could believe that it is haunted and, although I am sceptical, a photo I took during my visit showed up a strange anomaly, almost like the white shirt of a person passing a door. Of course, as pointed out by Kirsten, it could equally be a stain or light on the door. Whatever the case, I certainly didn't notice it at the time.

BETCHWORTH CASTLE
Surrey
....

www.dorkingmuseum.org.uk/local-history
/great-estates/betchworth-castle/

Now a crumbling ruin, Betchworth Castle is a shell of its former glory as a fortified medieval stone house. Built on a sandstone spur overlooking the western bank of the River Mole in Surrey, it is a Scheduled Ancient Monument.

Originally an earthwork fortress built by Robert Fitz Gilbert in the eleventh century, the castle was held by Richard de Tonbridge at the time of the Domesday Book. It was then granted to Richard FitzAlan in 1373 and his son, Sir John FitzAlan, turned it into a stone castle in 1379. It passed by marriage to Sir Thomas Browne, Sheriff of Kent, who rebuilt it in 1448 as a fortified house

In the nineteenth century, there was little practical use for castles, and Betchworth was abandoned in the 1830s. It was then bought in 1834, but the new owner demolished parts of it for reuse in other buildings. Without a permanent tenant, the remainder gradually fell into ruin and later became treated as a folly.

The castle is said to be haunted by a black devil-dog that prowls the ruins at night as well as the grounds of the castle, now Betchworth Park golf course.

Also known as devil-dogs or Black Shuck, among other names, black dogs are essentially a nocturnal specter and its appearance is often regarded as a portent of death. In general, they are much larger than a physical dog and are quite often reported as having large, glowing eyes and a silent gait. According to some legends, to see one three times will result in the witness dying an untimely and suspicious death. Not surprisingly they are often associated with moors, lonely back roads, and crossroads and in this case, the castle.

In addition, one owner, purported to be Lord Hope, chased and killed who he thought was an escaping convict with his sword. He later tragically discovered that it was in fact his own son he had killed. As a result, his remorseful ghost is said to wander the grounds.

BODIAM CASTLE

East Sussex

....

www.nationaltrust.org.uk/bodiam-castle

Built in 1385 by Sir Edward Dalyngrigge, a former knight of Edward III, Bodiam Castle is a fourteenth-century moated castle constructed to defend the area against French invasion during the Hundred Years' War. Built to a quadrangular plan, it has no keep, instead having its various chambers built around the outer defensive walls and inner courts. Its corners and entrance are marked by towers and topped by crenulations.

Now just a ruin, its structure, detail, and placement within an artificial water-surrounded landscape indicate that display was as important an aspect of the castle's design as defense. Indeed, although licensed for military defense, some believe the castle is nothing more than a fancy manor built to boost the reputation of its owner. Whatever the case, it is considered one of the last great medieval castles in England.

Although never involved in any war, Bodiam Castle houses a number of spectral entities like most medieval castles across the land. And as Richard Jones noted in his book *Haunted Castles of Britain and Ireland*, "Some people passing the ruins at dead of night have reported the distinctive sound of spectral revels emanating from the hollow shell. Others have told of hearing strange oaths and foreign-sounding songs."

As well, there is a mysterious red lady who is sometimes seen gazing from one of the towers, her eyes fixed upon some distant unknown object. Although quite famous, no one is quite sure who she is.

Another mysterious spirit involves a little boy dressed in clothes that appear to be straight out of a Dickens novel. His ghost was seen in 1994 running toward the castle but vanished midway across the bridge, suggesting he may have fallen into the moat and drowned. As with the Red lady, nothing else is known about him.

DONNINGTON CASTLE
Berkshire

....

www.english-heritage.org.uk/visit/places/donnington-castle

A ruined medieval castle in the English county of Berkshire, it was founded by Sir Richard Abberbury the Elder in 1386 and at one stage was bought by Thomas Chaucer before being taken under royal control during the Tudor period. During the first English civil war, the castle was held by the Royalists and endured an eighteen-month siege, after which the garrison eventually surrendered. The castle was subsequently demolished in 1646 and only the substantial four towered gatehouse survives as a scheduled ancient monument.

The castle and its grounds are reputed to be haunted by several different ghosts. The gatehouse itself is home to the ghost of a guard who appears in solid form and suddenly vanishes. He has been seen on both floors of the gatehouse and is often mistaken for a guide in period dress. A ghostly reenactment of a skirmish between a Royalist cavalry patrol from the castle and a parliamentary force has also been reported, while in 1990 several visitors witnessed the apparition of a white dog running down the hill from the castle toward the woods where it promptly vanished before reaching the tree line.

The ghostly form of "the Green Lady," thought to be Lady Hoby, who once lived there has also been seen by the castle gates. She is said to ask visitors why the gates are closed, before suddenly disappearing. And in another distressing encounter, a group of campers witnessed the apparition of an elderly Royalist soldier with a young woman in a headlock and pulling her hair. Alarmed by this, one of the campers yelled out to leave her alone to which the apparition simply growled. As such, the group approached the two phantoms and were shocked when they simply vanished before their eyes.

DOVER CASTLE

Kent

....

www.english-heritage.org.uk/visit/places/dover-castle

Overlooking the sea from a commanding and intimidating position, Dover Castle is situated at the shortest sea-crossing of the English Channel, which made it one of the most important defensive sites in Britain. Built in the twelfth century, records show there has been a fortified site at this location since Saxon times, and its crucial defensive position has seen it often referred to as the "Key to England."

Built to guard England's shores from pirates and in later years, Napoleon's army, it is now best known for its role in the Second World War and its secret underground command center, which was often frequented by Winston Churchill.

In May 1940, Admiral Sir Bertram Ramsey directed Operation Dynamo, the evacuation of French and British soldiers from Dunkirk from headquarters in the cliff tunnels below the castle, and a military telephone exchange was installed in 1941 to serve the underground headquarters.

These days the castle is a Scheduled Monument and is a major tourist attraction. However, it holds more than just historical fascination for many. Indeed, for the ghost hunter or paranormal investigator, it is a veritable treasure trove with a number of ghostly occurrences being recorded at the site including the headless ghost of a drummer boy, possibly from Napoleonic times, who haunts the battlements. It is said that he was decapitated and robbed during an errand that involved a large sum of money. His spirit has been seen numerous times across the castle grounds, and his forlorn drumming is said to ring out at various times.

And not surprisingly for a structure of such age and historical turmoil, disembodied voices have been heard during the night, sudden unexplained drops in temperature have been recorded, and witnesses have reported doors opening and closing of their own accord. On one occasion a camera crew that was filming at the castle keep heard a loud scream from the battlements above, as if someone had thrown themselves or fallen over the edge. Thoroughly convinced that someone was falling toward them, they ran for cover only to realize that when the scream stopped, no body hit the ground.

Deep within the stone walls of the old keep the apparition of a cavalier has been seen, as well as a woman in a red dress. In the underground tunnels the ghosts of Second World War soldiers have made their presence felt as they endlessly go about their daily duties, as if unaware that the war ceased many decades ago. And it was in these areas that an American couple once had the fright of their life when they heard violent screams and cries for help. After settling down they consoled themselves by believing it to be part of a reenactment, only to be later chilled to the bone when they were told there were no events happening that day.

On one occasion, a group of schoolchildren were sketching in the tunnels. When they handed in their pieces of paper, one boy had written "Where is Helen?", and when questioned, he told staff he had met a man in the tunnels dressed in a green jumper and brown trousers who was looking for a woman called Helen. A search was carried out but no one matching Helen was found. Neither, apparently, was the man in the green jumper and brown trousers, a dress that reminds one somewhat of a Second World War officer.

On another occasion, visitors on a guided tour reported that a door had suddenly slammed shut and a stretcher trolley exhibit had moved rapidly along the corridor, as if violently being pushed.

In September 2014, *The Daily Mirror* reported that a ghost, or what seemed to be a ghost, was caught on camera at the entrance to the historic castle. In a clip that lasts just over a minute, a dark wispy figure can be seen slowly walking across the entrance before disappearing; however, what makes it even more fascinating is the fact that the camera also picks up a bemused security guard as he searches for the figure.

FARNHAM CASTLE
Surrey
....
www.farnhamcastle.com

The North View of Farnham Castle, in the County of Surry.

Originally built in 1138 by Henri de Blois, Bishop of Winchester and grandson of William the Conqueror, the castle was the home of the Bishops of Winchester for over eight hundred years.

The original building was demolished by Henry II in 1155 and then rebuilt in the late twelfth and early thirteenth centuries. In the early fifteenth century it was the home of Cardinal Henry Beaufort, who presided at the trial of Joan of Arc in 1414. After the Civil War in 1648, the castle was again destroyed but was rebuilt and added to by Bishop George Morley in the seventeenth century.

During the Second World War, the castle was the location of the Camouflage Development and Training Center and for the last fifty plus years has been an intercultural training and conference center

Witnesses visiting the twelft- century keep have reported seeing a ghostly male figure in a long garment that simply disappears into thin air when confronted. It is believed that this is the spirit of Bishop Morley, who apparently led a very simple life. He is also said to haunt Waynflete's Tower, while the Great Hall is said to be haunted by the ghost of a young girl who, legend says, was forced to dance until she dropped dead. Some witnesses have reported seeing her ghostly figure, while others have reported hearing her tiny footsteps on the floor.

The staircase at the castle is also said to be haunted, again by Morley as well as by a monk in gray robes who is often seen gliding down the staircase and looking more flesh and blood than ghost. A shadowy figure has been witnessed in the area of the gateway, ramparts and keep, and the ghostly apparition of a stern lady in a light-colored gown has also been witnessed. It is believed that she originates from the twelfth century.

In addition, it has been often reported by town folk that they have heard bells ringing out for Waynflete's Tower, even though the Tower hasn't had bells in it for years. To add to this, the moat is said to be haunted by a procession of ghostly monks who appear extremely lifelike but then disappear. Even creepier, children have been heard on a number of occasions and voices reported coming from the Great Hall when no one has been in there.

Recently a security guard on patrol reported hearing mumbling and talking from the Great Hall. However, when he arrived there was no one there even though the talking continued. Apparently the guard exited the room and decided on doing outdoor patrols for that night. As well, a resident manager was sleeping overnight and awoke to see children standing at the end of the bed in medieval dress. Children have been seen and heard running along the length of the upper balcony, as if playing. It is also rumored that, in the cellar, a soldier who was shot in the face causes visitors to experience face-aches.

Peter Underwood, in his book *Haunted Farnham*, recalls meeting a person who was invited to spend a night at the castle. Underwood noted, "She told me she slept in an older part of the building and during the night found herself suddenly wide awake with the terrifying feeling that someone was in the room. She then felt her bedclothes being slowly pulled off her bed. Frightened, but aware of what was happening, she took a firm hold of the bedclothes and to her horror found that she had to exert considerable strength to keep the sheet and blanket from being drawn away from her.

"As she turned on her side to get a better hold on the bedclothes, she became aware that she could see 'something' in the corner of the bedroom. It seemed to have no definite shape but looked like someone crouching, huddled in the darkness, pulsating almost, exuding a sense of evil. After what seemed a long time struggling with the bedclothes and watching the unpleasant shape in the corner of the room, although it was probably only a few moments—or even seconds—the frightened visitor became aware that the dark form was no longer in the corner of the room and suddenly the bedclothes were no longer being tugged off the bed."

Not surprisingly, after that experience she said that nothing would induce her to ever stay another night in the castle.

HASTINGS CASTLE

East Sussex

....

www.discoverhastings.co.uk

In 1066, William the Conqueror arrived in England and ordered three fortifications to be built: Pevensey Castle, Hastings Castle, and Dover Castle. Like most early Norman fortresses, Hastings Castle was originally a motte-and-bailey, which was later rebuilt in stone, and for most of the Norman period the castle was held by the Count of Eu.

Ferocious storms battered the south coast for many months in 1287 and the sandstone cliffs and parts of the castle fell into the sea. Throughout the following centuries, erosion continued and more and more of the castle was lost.

During World War II, the castle received more damage, as Hastings was a target for German bombing raids. However, in 1951 the Hastings Corporation purchased the ruined site and converted it into a popular tourist attraction.

The ghost of Thomas Becket, who was thought to have been the church's dean at one time, is said to wander the castle ruins and in an area known as The Ladies Parlour, where it is believed tournaments were held. It is said that the manifestation of a lady dressed in a shimmering white gown can still be seen on moonlit nights. The dungeons, known as the "Whispering Dungeons" took their name from the fact that prisoners were overheard talking by guards who were several yards away in another room, are also said to be haunted with the ghostly sounds of prisoners rattling their chains and calling out for food, while the ghost of a nun or cloaked woman has been seen on the West Hill.

Another ghostly woman carrying a child is seen—it is said that she was deserted by her lover, so she opted to end her life as well as her child's by committing suicide. Apart from that, the ghost of a nun haunts the castle and the upper floors of the castle are subjected to phantom organ music. As well, a World War I nurse is said to haunt the nearby Wallingers Walk.

HERSTMONCEUX CASTLE

East Sussex

....

www.herstmonceux-castle.com

A stunning fairy tale–like castle that seemingly floats upon its moat, Herstmonceux Castle was built by Thomas Fiennes shortly after the Battle of Agincourt in the 1440s. It is one of the oldest significant brick buildings still standing in England, and although imposing, it was built more for its aesthetic qualities than defensive.

The Fiennes family maintained an important position at court for a century before Lord Thomas Dacre, had a disagreement with Henry VIII and was implicated in a murder. He was executed at Tyburn in 1541, and Henry seized the castle and estate. However, it was returned to the family when Elizabeth I came to power.

The castle remained untouched during the English Civil War, but by 1777 was in a state of disrepair due to the Fiennes' profligate lifestyle and spending. It became a romantic, ivy-covered ruin and a popular destination for day-trippers. From 1957 to 1988 it became the home of the Royal Observatory, Greenwich and today it is used by the Bader International Study Centre of Queen's University, Canada.

The ghost of a twenty-year-old woman haunts the castle moat. She is seen either swimming or standing beside the water and according to locals she drowned there on the eve of her twenty-first birthday. As well, the ghost of a Grey Lady is seen in the castle. It is thought that she is Grace Naylor, who was starved to death at the castle in 1727.

Additionally, a phantom drummer who emits a blue spark on every beat and who is said to be nine feet tall also haunts the battlements. He is thought to be the ghost of a drummer from the battle of Agincourt. Local legend suggests that the eccentric lord hammered on a drum in order to keep lovers away from his young wife. She eventually became so annoyed with him that she locked him in a tiny room and left him to die. The sound of his drum could still be heard long after his death and kept her lovers away.

A ghostly lady is often reported riding a white donkey around the castle grounds while the ghost of a White Lady has also been reported in the grounds of the castle. Legend says that she was lured to the castle by Sir Roger de Fienes, who raped her and then had her killed. Her ghost has been seen walking around the grounds of the castle's moat in a distressed state. She has also been seen inside the castle close to the gatehouse. A phantom horse rider has also been reported galloping across nearby fields and is presumed to be Lord Dacre.

HEVER CASTLE

Kent

....

www.hevercastle.co.uk

Hever Castle was built around 1270 and first consisted of a walled bailey surrounded by a moat. However, in 1460, Henry Bullen, a wealthy London merchant, purchased the castle and converted it to a Tudor dwelling. His son Thomas changed his surname to Boleyn and later married Elizabeth Howard, the daughter of the Duke of Norfolk.

Together the two had many children, one being Anne Boleyn, whose name is now synonymous with the quaint stone building. Anne, who later married Henry VIII, was arrested and charged with adultery and incest and was sentenced to death at the Tower of London. She was beheaded on May 19, 1536.

It is Anne's ghost who seems to haunt this most beautiful and evocative building. Indeed, one could even suggest that her spirit is one of the most, if not the most, reported ghosts of all time. Interestingly, as we have previously seen regarding the Tower of London, Anne's ghost not only appears at Hever but also Blickling Hall in Norfolk, Rochford Hall in Essex, and as we shall see, Windsor Castle as well.

In May 2010, I was fortunate enough to spend a good half day at the castle, wandering its grounds and exploring its magnificent hallways, stairwells, and rooms, including the room rumored to be that of Anne's—a bedroom she shared with her sister Mary. The bedroom itself is somehow atmospheric as if history itself seeps from its stone walls and dark timber furniture. Leaning against the fireplace one cannot help but realize that Anne herself must have done the same at some stage. Indeed, looking out the window is to see the landscape that Anne must have loved so much as a child, albeit, restored and remodeled over the years.

It is quiet and peaceful at this time, I have somehow luckily escaped the crowds for this moment, and for an instant I am able to be alone in this truly splendid place. I gaze out of the window at the lush green lawns and mature trees that sit serenely in the warmth and sunlight of an early English summer. Turning around I feel as if someone or something is in the room with me, as if watching quietly from a corner, unseen and unheard. But of course, there is no one there, and soon my serenity is broken by the arrival of a family with day packs and cameras and noisy children. The moment is gone, whatever ghosts that haunt this room have gone. And yet, for a fleeting moment, one could believe they exist.

Anne's ghostly apparition has been seen wandering the gardens of the castle, often drifting over the bridge that crosses the River Eden. As well, her figure has been reported in what is thought to have been her bedroom. Is it too much of a stretch to suggest that her restless spirit has returned to a place where she spent many happy years, and from where she began her journey that would change the face of history for England?

Other ghosts at Hever Castle include a despondent spirit of unknown origin who wanders the gallery, often groaning and banging. As well, a phantom horse has also been seen, oddly enough, galloping through the long gallery.

In 2015 a tourist, Liam Archer, who was visiting the castle, captured an eerie image of what he claimed is the ghost of Anne Boleyn stalking the corridors. After spending an afternoon at the castle with his family and taking various photographs including one of an ornate fireplace in a dimly-lit living room, Archer he took the picture which appears to show something out of the ordinary.

Unaware of it at the time, he was surprised to find what looked like a hovering hand with a long finger apparently pointing towards the chimney. He noted afterward, "In the prayer room there was a fog or a mist hovering around, but I didn't think much of it at the time. I felt like an unknown force was pulling me through the castle. I couldn't see it, but I could definitely feel it. I didn't know what to make of it because I didn't believe in ghosts at this point. But I am now confident it is her."

LEEDS CASTLE
Kent

....

www.leeds-castle.com

With a site dating back to 857, one would think Leeds Castle in Kent, some five miles southeast of Maidstone, would be teeming with ghosts and ghostly stories. However, contrary to this, if anything, it appears quiet in supernatural phenomena.

A stunning and imposing fortress of stone seemingly floating on a shallow lake, and invoking visions of the Arthurian Avalon, my partner Kirsten and I visited the castle on a day when the sun shone merrily through high wispy clouds and the day was warm. The scent of an English spring wafted pleasantly past our nostrils and small sparrow like birds twittered incessantly in the bushes and hedgerows.

To reach the castle you must park your car and then walk along a crunchy gravel path that winds its way through stunning gardens of beautifully manicured lawns, regimented hedges, and imposing trees. The visitors then follow the path as it runs parallel to a small brook that cheerfully babbles its way through this wonderful landscape. If you are lucky you may run into the resident peacocks or spy a fat pike lurking in the shallows.

A castle has been on the site since 1119 and was used by King Edward I in the thirteenth century, while Henry VIII used it as a residence for his first wife, Catherine of Aragon, in the sixteenth century. These days the castle dates mostly from the nineteenth century and is built on the islands in a lake formed by the River Len. Known as a 'ladies castle' and for its stunningly beautiful location, it is a popular tourist attraction and has been open to the public since the mid-1970s.

Surprisingly, the main ghost that is said to haunt Leeds is not a vague woman in red or white or even a ghostly cavalier, instead it is a black dog which is said can appear and disappear within moments, sometimes fading into a wall or passing through closed doors. The dog is said to terrorize the castle grounds and has become associated with a death or other misfortune befalling a member of the castle owner's family.

Interestingly, one story that is widely believed contradicts this beast-of-misfortune legend as many years ago a woman was sitting by a window when she saw the spectral dog disappearing into a wall. The woman went to investigate when the window by which she had been sitting suddenly collapsed, the bricks and rubble landing on the spot where she had been just moments before.

The origin of the ghostly dog is said to lie in the witchcraft dabbling of Henry VI's aunt, Eleanor of Gloucester, who in 1431 was found guilty of practicing necromancy, witchcraft, heresy, and treason. As a result, she was imprisoned at Leeds Castle for life. Some have speculated that the dog may have been cursed in some way and as such is doomed to haunt the castle forever.

Apart from that, witnesses have also reported seeing a ghostly woman gliding along the corridors of the castle, and she is believed to be none other than the Duchess of Gloucester herself. As well, the apparition of a woman in a long flowing dress brushing her hair has also been seen in the grounds and in the Queen's Room

More recently the ghosts of two other dogs have been reported, a small white dog and a much larger black dog. They are believed to have been the pets of Lady Baillie, an Anglo-American heiress and previous owner of the castle, who owned a small terrier called Smudge and a Great Dane called Boots.

Interestingly, although not a classic ghost sighting, an incident regarding a so called time-slip has been reported from the castle when a woman, Alice Pollock, was touching objects in the Henry VIII's rooms in an attempt to experience events from another time. After a short period of receiving no impressions, she reported that the room suddenly changed, losing its modern, comfortable appearance and becoming cold and bare. The carpet had disappeared and there were now logs burning on the fire, while a tall woman in a white dress was walking up and down the room; her face appearing to be in deep concentration. Not long after the room returned to its original state.

Later research showed that the rooms had been the prison of Queen Joan of Navarre, Henry V's stepmother after she had been accused of witchcraft by her husband.

OXFORD CASTLE
Oxfordshire

....

www.oxfordcastleunlocked.co.uk

Oxford Castle lies in the heart of Oxfordshire with a history dating as far back as the Norman Conquest of England. First built by Robert D'Oyly the Elder, it is somewhat surprisingly not among the forty-eight castles recorded in the Domesday Book of 1086. However, it must be noted that for all its remarkable detail, not every castle in existence at the time was recorded in the survey.

D'Oyly arrived in England with William the Conqueror during the Norman Conquest of England in 1066. Later

William granted him lands in Oxfordshire, and as Oxford had suffered considerable damage during the invasion, D'Oyly was directed by William to construct a castle to control the town.

Originally a moated, wooden motte-and-bailey, the castle was replaced in stone in the eleventh century and played an important role in the Conflict of the Anarchy, a civil war in England and Normandy between 1135 and 1153, which resulted in a widespread breakdown in law and order. However, in the fourteenth century the site became used primarily for county administration and as a prison. During the English Civil War, most of the castle was destroyed, and by the eighteenth century, the remaining buildings where converted into Oxford's local prison. A new prison complex was built on the site from 1785, which became HM Prison Oxford. In 1996 the prison closed and was redeveloped as a hotel with the medieval remains of the castle, including the motte, St George's Tower, and the crypt being Grade I buildings as well as Scheduled Monuments.

And with such a history of execution, murder, hardship, depravity, and intense fighting, it is hardly surprising that the castle is one of the most haunted in England, with people reporting dark shadowy figures, poltergeist activity and more.

The ghostly figure of a woman has been seen walking the Castle Mound, and many believe that this is the restless spirit of Mary Blandy, who was executed for murder at the castle in 1752. In addition, it was reported that sometime in the 1970s a paranormal investigation group was carrying out a séance in one of the cells when poltergeist activity suddenly began to occur—things getting so bad that a priest had to be called to exorcise whatever strange entity they had accidentally summoned.

Disembodied footsteps are also often heard around the prison wing corridor, and an amorphous white mist has often been reported rising up a flight of stairs only to disappear once it reaches the top.

However, perhaps the most frightening report came from some security guards who were on a nightly patrol. Security staff at the castle have long reported many strange things, such as unexplained sounds, bangs, and disembodied voices. However, one night a guard was coming to the end of his patrol when his dog stopped and quickly backed up, growling at something in front of him. Then, as the guard tried to calm the dog, two large shadowy figures appeared before him. Terrified, he immediately ran in the opposite direction to escape whatever it was. Sadly, it was reported that the dog died a few days later, apparently frightened to death.

In March 2014, Tim Stanley wrote in the *Telegraph* of a ghost hunt he attended at the castle with Dr. Ciarán O'Keeffe, a lecturer in parapsychology. Stanley, who claims to have witnessed a ghost when he was ten years old recalled that while alone in the crypt he, "suddenly found that I was not alone. How to describe it? It was similar to the feeling that you might get when your eyes are closed and someone walks into the room. You cannot hear or see them, but you know that they are there. I knew that standing to my right-hand side was a little girl. I couldn't see her or touch her and she said nothing. But she was there."

Later O'Keeffe clarified the situation by stating that "Some mediums have, in the past few months, said that they think there is a little girl in the crypt, too."

To this day, the original motte, crypt, and St George's Tower remain and are a popular, if grim, location for paranormal investigations and ghost tours.

PEVENSEY CASTLE

East Sussex

....

www.english-heritage.org.uk/visit/places/pevensey-castle

Built around 290 AD and known to the Romans as Anderitum, Pevensey Castle is a medieval castle and former Roman Saxon Shore fort. It is a Scheduled Monument and is long thought to have been originally built as a Roman defense to guard the British coastline from Saxon pirates.

Anderitum fell into ruin following the end of the Roman occupation but was reoccupied in 1066 by the Normans. A stone keep and fortifications were built within the old Roman walls and although it was twice starved into surrender, it was never successfully stormed. It was generally occupied until the sixteenth century when it became abandoned until it was acquired by the state in 1925. Between 1940 and 1945 it was garrisoned by units from the Home Guard, the British and Canadian armies, and the United States Army Air Corps, and machine-gun posts were built into the Roman and Norman walls. These emplacements can still be seen today.

The most famous ghost that haunts the castle is "The Lady in White." She has apparently appeared a number of times in the surrounding fields. Indeed, it was reported that one summer's evening a few years ago a group of twelve campers were putting up their tents in a field adjacent to the castle when one of them saw, in the next field, what he thought was an old lady dressed in a long white raincoat that came down to her ankles. He then realized that she wasn't walking but gliding and so called his friends and they all watched her float up the hill toward the castle, at one stage passing right through a wooden fence. They decided to give chase; however, as they got close to the strange apparition, it drifted into some bushes. The campers surrounded the bushes but found no sign of anyone. This was enough for them and they packed up and left.

In addition to this, a "gray or pale lady" is said to haunt the ruined interior of the castle. She has been seen slowly pacing up and down one of the parapets and there has been some speculation as to her identity with some suggesting that she is Lady Joan Pelham, whose husband took over the castle in 1394. When he was called away to fight a battle in the north, Lady Pelham was left at Pevensey in charge of the castle. With the majority of soldiers gone, the castle was besieged by an invading army demanding its surrender in the name of King Richard II.

Lady Pelham, now trapped in her own castle, not only feared for her own life but also that of her husband's. She managed to hold on, later pacing the parapet every day until he returned. However, it was said that she suffered a great deal of mental trauma from the siege, and this is the reason that her restless and troubled spirit still walks the battlements.

Others, however, suggest that the spirit is that of Queen Joan of Navarre, wife of Henry IV and stepmother to Henry V. She was falsely charged with witchcraft and later held in custody at Pevensey Castle in 1419. She was released several years later when Henry V reprieved her, apparently feeling remorse for the ill-treatment she received, something she apparently never got over.

Other sightings include a Roman centurion marching on the castle battlements, and the ghost of a drummer boy who, according to locals, is still beating out the alarm of a Saxon attack. A number of people have reported that they have heard the sounds of marching soldiers and the screams and moans of dying men drifting across to the castle from the site of the 1066 Battle of Hastings, while a black monk has been sighted in a nearby valley. Interestingly, it is suspected that this ghost is of a relatively recent origin, as much of the land in that area around the castle was covered by the sea until only a few hundred years ago.

More recently, a local resident of the area claimed to have seen a ghost three days in a row, each time at six in the morning while walking his dog. Apparently the man would walk his dog every morning before work and on one of these days he noticed someone dressed in black on the far side of a field. Thinking that it was someone else out for an early walk he gave it no thought; however, he saw the same figure the very next day and again on a third successive day. Picking up a stick and throwing it for the dog to retrieve, the wind caught the stick and blew it toward the figure, landing behind it. To the astonishment of the owner, the dog ran straight through the body of the black figure.

Frightened by what he had witnessed, the man left the field immediately but returned again the next morning. However, he never saw the black figure again.

PORTCHESTER CASTLE
Hampshire
....

www.english-heritage.org.uk/visit/places/portchester-castle

Portchester Castle is located at the northern end of Portsmouth Harbour in Hampshire. It is a medieval castle built within a former Roman fort. Believed to have been founded in the late eleventh century, Portchester was a baronial castle and was a favored hunting lodge of King John. In 1216 it was besieged and captured by the French, although not held for any great length of time before being retaken and returned to English control

The castle itself occupies a commanding position at the head of Portsmouth Harbour and, in anticipation of a French invasion during the first part of the fourteenth century, Edward II repaired and reinforced its already daunting battlements.

In 1632 the castle was sold to Sir William Uvedale. Since then, it has passed through a number of his successors and, although it did not witness fighting during the English Civil War, it was garrisoned by Parliamentarian dragoons in 1644, mounted infantry who were trained in horse riding as well as infantry fighting skills.

However, the castle is renowned these days as being a prison, one of its common uses especially from the late seventeenth century onward when it took on this important function in a full-time capacity. In 1665, some five-hundred prisoners from the second Anglo-Dutch war were held within its towering walls and between 1702 and 1712 the Crown leased Portchester Castle from its owners to imprison prisoners from the Spanish War of Succession.

It was last used as a gaol in the nineteenth century for over 7000 French prisoners of the Napoleonic Wars. Those unfortunate souls that died in captivity were often buried in what are now the tidal mudflats to the south of the castle, and their remains occasionally rise from the mud when disturbed by storms.

Today Portchester Castle is a Scheduled Ancient Monument and a Grade I building, and although appearing quiet by the standards of many haunted English castles, is still reputed to be haunted by several ghosts—a black monk and a spectral horseman seen riding through the grounds. Indeed, with regards to the latter, in one encounter Sheila Sayce, an employee leading a tour of the grounds, was convinced she witnessed a ghostly black horse and rider. She noted; "As it grew in size, it started to come towards me and I screamed and ran away. My colleague saw it over my shoulder too—it was a long, low, jet black shape with four legs and a horse's head and it projected a very bad feeling."

Sayce also noted "The following year a young lad came in with a video. He had been larking around outside the castle late one night and wanted to know if we could identify a strange sound on the tape. It was the sound of horse's hooves on concrete."

There has also been evidence of satanic witchcraft rituals found within the graveyard which sits within the castle walls. As well, a woman who fell to her death while trying to rescue her baby is said to roam the grounds, as does the spirit of a girl who was said to have thrown herself off the walls in the seventeenth century after hearing of the death of her fiancé at sea.

Interestingly, local legend suggests that Pontius Pilate visited here late in his life although, obviously, the current castle would not have existed at this time.

It is truly a spectacular place to visit, something I did in the early summer of 2010, and although I didn't witness anything of a supernatural nature, I am not surprised that tales of ghost's comings-and-goings abound from this incredible site.

ROCHESTER CASTLE
Kent

....

www.english-heritage.org.uk/visit/places/rochester-castle

Situated on the River Medway and Watling Street, Rochester Castle served as an important royal castle and helped protect England's south-east coast from invasion during the late-medieval period.

The first castle at Rochester was founded just after the Norman Conquest. It was given to Bishop Odo, probably by his half-brother William the Conqueror.

During the Rebellion of 1088 over the succession to the English throne, Odo supported Robert Curthose, William's eldest son, against William Rufus and the castle first saw military action when both the city and castle were besieged after Odo made Rochester a headquarters for the rebellion. Afterward the first castle was abandoned.

Between 1087 and 1089, Rufus built a new stone castle at Rochester, and although much altered these days, some of the original parts still remain. The twelfth-century keep or stone tower, which is the castle's most prominent feature, is one of the best preserved in England.

The ghost of Lady Blanche de Warenne has been seen walking the castle battlements, protruding from her chest the arrow that accidentally killed her at Easter in 1264. According to legend, the arrow was tragically fired by her betrothed in an attempt to protect her from the unwanted attentions of another man—the arrow bouncing off the armor of its intended target and striking Lady Blanche, killing her instantly.

Another ghostly woman, or possibly the same, has also been regularly reported. In December 2007 a visitor reported seeing a lady in medieval garments walking down a spiral staircase in the castle before walking through a wall and disappearing, while in 2010 another visitor to the castle reported that, while in the gallery, they distinctly heard a woman whisper in their ear. In 2010 another visitor reported seeing a transparent figure in one of the upper floors and that it walked through an archway and then across thin air as though there was still a floor in place.

A fact sheet given out by staff states: "In the chapel, which now has the model of the castle in it, and directly above the shop, which would have originally been the fore building, there is a presence of a man, possibly a man of the cloth (priest)."

In February 2008, a tall dark figure was seen by a witness who became extremely distressed. During the same year another witness reported hearing "footsteps behind me and (I) looked around and in the shadows I saw a hooded figure that said in no uncertain terms, 'Get out!'"

Oddly enough, a couple visiting the castle earlier that year reported that "My husband and I were walking around the middle section of the castle when, without warning, it went icy cold all around us and we both heard a voice, in a whispery rasp say, 'Go away!'"

In 2009 another couple reportedly noted a drop in temperature and the same voice saying the same words, while another visitor reported seeing a monk in the chapel. Strangely, another couple in the room at the same time failed to see the apparition.

Neil Arnold, in his book *Haunted Rochester* also notes that, in 2006, a married couple visiting the castle were alarmed by a sudden white fog which appeared near the ladder to the cesspit, while in October of the same year, a man with white hair was seen gazing out of one of the unoccupied windows. In June 2007 a man reported that he'd seen a strange mist and two orb like objects emerging from the well. Arnold also reports that in 2010 some visitors from Iceland encountered two men dressed in medieval attire but, upon later enquiring of them, were told that there were no re-enactments at the castle that day.

The ghost of an old man, thought to be that of Charles Dickens, has been seen near the Old Burial Ground by the castle moat. Dickens was said to have loved Rochester and expressed a wish to be buried there, however, after his death he was interred in Westminster Abbey as this was considered the only place suitable for such a great author. Whatever the case, it appears that Rochester Castle is a place where encountering supernatural spirits is not unusual.

SISSINGHURST CASTLE

Kent

....

www.nationaltrust.org.uk/sissinghurst-castle

Although Sissinghurst is technically not a castle, contemporary records suggest that the site was occupied by a moated manor house in the late twelfth century and by the middle of the thirteenth century belonged to the de Bereham family who held it until Henry de Bereham sold it to Thomas Baker in the late 1400s. The Bakers, however, backed the Royalists during the English Civil War and by the late seventeenth century the place was in serious decline. From 1756 to 1763 it was let to the government as a military prison also resulting in considerable damage.

These days it is owned and maintained by the National Trust and is among the most famous gardens in England, being created in the 1930s by Vita Sackville-West, poet and gardening writer, and her husband Harold (later Sir Harold) Nicolson, an author and diplomat. It is, of course, reputed to be haunted.

A number of unnamed ghosts are said to haunt Sissinghurst Castle, most of which appear to stem from the time of Queen Mary's reign when Sir John Baker resided in the castle. Sir John was known for the execution of hundreds of Protestants and was referred to as "Bloody Baker" and was rumored to have murdered a local priest whose ghost now wanders the grounds. The priest, who legend suggests was bricked up alive in one of the buildings walls, is often heard by visitors, his eerie disembodied footsteps walking beside them on the crunchy gravel paths. Indeed, famed ghost hunter Peter Underwood noted, "In the 1950s, Felix Seward, Chairman of the Ghost Club from 1954 to 1960, knew both Sir Harold and Lady Nicolson and, knowing of his great interest in psychic matters, they talked freely to him about the ghost priest."

Underwood added that on one occasion, while speaking with Sir Harold over lunch, he was told that the priest had been seen, heard, and felt on numerous occasions, even by Sir Harold himself. This was backed up by the housekeeper, a Mrs. Hayter, who reported that many visitors had asked her whom the "reverend gentleman" was who was lurking around the place.

Underwood also suggests that Sir Harold himself now may haunt the place, noting that, "Sir Harold had the occasional habit of clicking his teeth with his tongue—and oddly, since his death a peculiar clicking noise has been heard in some of the rooms in the house."

WINDSOR CASTLE
Berkshire

....

www.royalcollection.org.uk/visit/windsorcastle

11379—Guard at Windsor Castle, Windsor, England.

Built by William the Conqueror in 1066, Windsor Castle was originally a timber motte-and-bailey structure designed to protect Norman authority around the outskirts of London and to protect a strategically important part of the River Thames. The earliest mention of Windsor is in the Anglo-Saxon Chronicle and comes from the English word *windlesore,* which means "winch by the riverside".

The castle was gradually replaced with stone fortifications over the years and withstood a prolonged siege during the First Barons' War at the start of the thirteenth century. Later, Henry III built a luxurious royal palace within the castle during the middle of the century, while Edward III further refurbished and rebuilt the palace to become what was described as the "most expensive secular building project of the entire Middle Ages in England." During the sixteenth century, Henry VIII and Elizabeth I used the castle predominantly as a royal court.

Surviving the English Civil War, when it was used as a military headquarters for Parliamentary forces and a prison for Charles I, it was later rebuilt again, this time by Charles II, and after a period of neglect during the eighteenth century, George III and George IV renovated once again. Queen Victoria later made a few minor changes to the castle, which became the center for royal entertainment for much of her reign. During the Second World War it became a place of refuge for the royal family during the Luftwaffe bombing campaigns. In 1992 it survived a devastating fire. Today it is the largest inhabited castle in the world, with more than 500 people living and working within its forbidding walls.

The castle has stood for nearly a thousand years in one form or another, and not surprisingly, it has many ghostly stories to tell, including that of the ghost of Henry VIII, who is said to be one of the most famous otherworldly inhabitants of the castle. Numerous people, including employees and visitors, report having heard the king in the cloisters. As well, he has also been seen wandering the corridors, moaning in pain and dragging his ulcerated leg behind him, an infection that greatly contributed to his death in 1547. He is often described by witnesses as a large and angry ghost irately pacing and occasionally shouting.

Anne Boleyn, who we have already seen seems to haunt a number of places, is another of the castle's many resident ghosts. The second wife of Henry VIII and beheaded in the Tower of London in 1536, her ghost is reported to haunt the Dean's Cloister at the castle and she had been seen numerous times peering through a window, her face drawn and distressed and sometimes weeping.

Elizabeth I, the youngest daughter of Henry VIII, has also been seen on numerous occasions, generally in the Royal Library, with people reporting hearing the sound of her high heels on the floorboards. She has also been seen a number of times at a window in the Dean's Cloister wearing a black gown and a back shawl.

As well, the ghost of King George III, who was often restricted to the castle, especially during his periods of madness, is said to appear in the library, peering mournfully through the windows and doorways.

And not surprisingly for a building of such age and history, there are numerous places within the castle walls that are reputed to be haunted by a number of unknown, or unnamed ghosts, such as the Curfew Tower, the Deanery and the Prison Room.

Interestingly, the ghost of Queen Victoria is reputed to have been displeased with the renovations made to the castle by her grandson Edward VIII, in particular, the removal of a specific spruce tree. When workers came to remove the tree, a number of inexplicable events hampered the removal and some even claimed to see the ghost of the old matriarch waving her arms wildly.

THREE

SOUTH WEST ENGLAND

BERKELEY CASTLE

Gloucestershire

....

www.berkeley-castle.com

Dating back to the eleventh century, Berkeley Castle is a Grade I building and has remained within the Berkeley family since they rebuilt it in the twelfth century, except for a brief period of royal ownership by the Tudors. The first castle at Berkeley was a motte-and-bailey, built around 1067 by William FitzOsbern.

Interestingly, in the year 1215, the castle was the place where the West Country barons assembled en route to their clash with King John at Runnymede just before the signing of the Magna Carta. And just as interesting is that the castle witnessed one of the most horrific deaths in history when, following imprisonment in the castle dungeons, the deposed King Edward II was sentenced to death by Queen Isabella.

It was hoped that Edward's imprisonment in the damp, unhygienic dungeons would be enough to kill the king, but surprisingly, although he did suffer from various ailments, he did not die. As such, it was decided to dispose of him in a straight forward manner, and Edward was allegedly to suffer possibly the most horrific death of any British king in history. Firstly, he was pinned down on a table and a funnel was thrust into his rectum. After this, a red-hot poker was thrust up into his bowels, truly a most painful and prolonged death, if the legend is to be believed, as the account given to Parliament at the time was simply that Edward had met with a fatal accident.

Having noted this, it is said that Edward's excruciating screams can be heard throughout the castle on the anniversary of his death and the room in which this apparent grisly murder was carried out can be visited by the public today as can the adjacent deep dungeon in which he was held.

BERRY POMEROY CASTLE

Devon

....

*www.english-heritage.org.uk/visit/places
/berry-pomeroy-castle*

Reportedly one of the most haunted places in the British Isles, Berry Pomeroy Castle, once a majestic and imposing structure in South Devon, is now nothing more than a romantic ruin. Built in the late fifteenth century by the Pomeroy family who held the land since the eleventh century, it was sold to Edward Seymour, 1st Duke of Somerset in 1547 although it was abandoned in the late seventeenth century when the fourth baronet moved to Wiltshire.

During the nineteenth century the castle became renowned as a perfect example of the "picturesque" and it rapidly became a popular tourist attraction, something that has continued to the present day. It is also said to be the abode of numerous ghosts including the apparitions of a Blue Lady and a White Lady.

The Blue Lady is said to lure people into various parts of the castle until they become lost. It is believed that she is the ghost of the daughter of a Norman lord who was raped by her father, becoming pregnant with his baby, with the baby later being strangled by the father in the castle. Other stories suggest that it was actually the mother who strangled the child. Whatever the case, the Blue Lady has become the death portent of the Seymours.

The White Lady is said to be the soul of Margaret Pomeroy who was held captive in the castle dungeon by her own sister, Eleanor who was jealous of her. Reputedly starved to death, her restless soul haunts the dungeons of St. Margaret's Tower, often waving to visitors, possibly trying to alert them to her plight.

Strange disembodied voices and cold spots have been reported as well as strange lights that seem to have a mind of their own. There are also the apparitions of a lady wearing a gray dress and that of a Cavalier soldier.

CORFE CASTLE

Dorset

....

www.nationaltrust.org.uk/corfe-castle

Built by William the Conqueror and dating back to the eleventh century, Corfe Castle occupies a gap in the Purbeck Hills on the route between Wareham and Swanage on the Isle of Purbeck in Dorset. It was one of the first castles in England to be built partly using stone and underwent major structural changes in the twelfth and thirteenth centuries.

During the middle ages it was to become one of five Royal castles. King John is reputed to have kept the Crown Jewels there, along with twenty-two imprisoned Frenchmen who he had incarcerated in the dungeons but neglected to feed and water them. The distressing disembodied sounds of men in their death throws have been heard coming from within the castle walls.

In 1572, the castle was sold by Elizabeth I to Sir Christopher Hatton. Later, in 1635, Sir John Bankes, a staunch Royalist, acquired the castle and was the owner during the English Civil War. Bankes died soon after leaving his wife, Lady Bankes, to defend the castle against the Parliamentarians and, no matter what Cromwell's army threw at the castle, it remained unbowed. In the end, it was an act of treachery by Colonel Pitman, one of Lady Bankes personnel, which saw the castles defenses breached.

With food and supplies getting low, Colonel Pitman secretly opened the gate and Cromwell's men took the castle after a short struggle. The castle was confiscated then blown up by Cromwell's engineers and what remains today is pretty much how Cromwell's men left it.

It is said that Lady Bankes' ghost haunts the castle to this day. She is described as being dressed in white, with her head bowed, although some say she appears to be headless. Her ghost has been seen to walk the castle walls, then glide slowly down the hill to the stream which runs alongside the castles base.

The ghost of a Roundhead has been seen on occasions in the National Trust tearooms and stockroom close to the main gate, and the sound of a galloping phantom horse can be heard at the bottom castle hill. At night people have also reported seeing puzzling flashes of light that flit across the castle and a legion of Roman soldiers is said to haunt the track that runs down from the Purbeck Hills to the foot of the castle.

In May 2009, Don Goodwin, who has lived in Hastings for over twenty years, was out collecting worms for bait at about 1:30 am one night when he saw a ghostly figure. He stated, "I looked up and there's this chap standing in the middle of the field. I was thinking, *what's he doing here at this time of the morning?* He had a long cloak on with a very high collar. I thought that was very unusual. He also had a small floppy-browed hat and he looked just like one of those Cavaliers. I bent down to pick a few more worms up and then I got back up and he vanished. It was a long way from the perimeter of the field and he would have had to run at full tilt to get to the bushes. It didn't frighten me, but I didn't know where he would have just disappeared to."

Goodwin added that the figure must have seen him, as he had his flashlight on. He also described the ghost as tall and said he saw it move as if to pick something up. Who it is, no one knows.

DUNSTER CASTLE
Somerset
....

www.nationaltrust.org.uk/dunster-castle

Dunster Castle sits serenely above the town of Dunster in Somerset atop a steep tor. It is a former motte-and-bailey castle but now spends its days as a country house. First fortified in the late Anglo-Saxon period, it was fully fortified after the Norman Conquest when William de Mohun constructed a timber castle on the site. The Norman motte-and-bailey were later demolished to make way for a much more substantial stone castle and, over time, the castle was remodeled, expanded and modernized on numerous occasions by the Luttrell family who were lords of the manor from the fourteenth to the twentieth century

Although the medieval castle walls were mostly destroyed following a siege during the English Civil War, it was later rebuilt in the mid-1800s by Anthony Salvin an architect and expert of medieval buildings. Later, in 1944 with the death of Alexander Luttrell, the family was unable to afford the death duties due on the estate and the castle and surrounding lands were sold off although the family continued to live in the castle as tenants. In 1976 the family bequeathed the castle to the National Trust, and today it is a Grade I building and Scheduled Monument and operates as an extremely popular tourist attraction.

People have been reporting ghostly encounters at Dunster Castle for years and years, with the most famous ghosts being a Grey Lady and the Foot Guard who wears a three-pointed hat. These two manifest themselves as blurry shapes or faces. And yet they are not the only paranormal inhabitants within the gray stone walls as others have reported strange noises, chills, feelings of general unease and bright floating orbs.

To gain entry to the castle one must first pass through the magnificent gatehouse, where, to one side is an oubliette, some seven or so meters deep. Excavations of the oubliette unearthed a male skeleton, not an ordinary skeleton but one that was roughly seven feet tall and chained to the wall by his wrists and ankles. Local legend suggests that his remains still lie in-situ in the oubliette and although it is now completely sealed, people have reported hearing cries and whimpers from beneath the stone floor that now covers the grim pit.

The Grey Lady, as we have previously mentioned, is Dunster's most regularly seen ghost. She has been sighted in various areas around the castle including the billiard room, the library, and the corridor that flanks the two. However, she is most often reported on the main stairs that lead up from the entrance hall, and although no one is sure, it is suggested that she may have been an abused servant girl who later died in the castle.

The "Grey Lady" is not the only spirit that haunts this place. In the King Charles Bedroom, people complain about the atmosphere that some describe as unpleasant, almost as if being watched. Many visitors have refused to enter the room, claiming that it has a bad feeling. As well, the leather gallery is also said to be haunted with visitors and staff reporting the sounds of men shouting, heavy footsteps, and the slamming of doors long after the castle has been closed and the visitors have left. Others have claimed to have been tapped on the shoulder only to turn and find no one there, and it is said that a distinct cold spot moves around the room. Indeed, in one case a staff member was working in the room when she suddenly became aware of a chill. Turning around, she was confronted by the ghostly figure of a man dressed in a Royalist uniform. The figure then vanished before her eyes.

The old stable block is said to be haunted by a "Man in Green," while others have claimed to have seen floating green orbs at the far end of the stable block. As well, the storeroom is said to suffer from poltergeist like activity in that boxes, books and stock are often found strewn around the floor when staff open up in the morning.

FARLEIGH HUNGERFORD CASTLE

Somerset

....

www.english-heritage.org.uk/visit/places
/farleigh-hungerford-castle

Farleigh Hungerford Castle in Somerset was first constructed between 1377 and 1383 by Sir Thomas Hungerford. Built to a quadrangular design on the site of an existing manor house overlooking the River Frome, it was later extended by his son Sir Walter Hungerford, courtier to Henry V, with an additional outer court enclosing the parish.

The castle generally remained with the Hungerford family over the next two hundred years, despite periods during the War of the Roses in which it was held by the Crown. At the onset of the English Civil War in 1642, the castle was held by Sir Edward Hungerford, who declared his support for Parliament, becoming a leader of the Roundheads in Wiltshire. But the castle was seized by Royalist forces in 1643 and recaptured by the Parliamentarians in 1645. As a result, it escaped slighting, unlike numerous other castles in England.

Sir Edward Hungerford was the last member of the Hungerford family to hold the castle, but his gambling and profligate lifestyle forced him to sell the property in 1686. Sadly, by the eighteenth century, the castle fell into disrepair and in 1730 much of it was broken up for salvage.

It is a formidable place and the walls cast long ominous shadows, which suggest a particularly tragic past. And in this case, the walls do not lie; the castle does not disappoint in this regard.

In 1516 Walter's son, Edward inherited the estate and married a widow by the name of Agnes. However, with Edward's death in 1522, Lady Agnes Hungerford was arrested on suspicion of murder, specifically that she had him strangled and his body gruesomely burnt in the kitchen at the castle. She was subsequently found guilty and later hanged at Tyburn, a site synonymous with public executions for almost six hundred years and now not far from Marble Arch, one of central London's busiest corners.

The tragic ghost of Lady Agnes Hungerford is said to return on occasions and has been seen in the vicinity of the chapel at twilight, apparently a serene and beautiful figure that appears for the briefest of moments before vanishing.

LYDFORD CASTLE

Devon

....

www.english-heritage.org.uk/visit/places
/lydford-castle-and-saxon-town

Built in the late 1060s, the original Lydford Castle was constructed by the Normans to control the inhabitants of Devon. This was followed in 1195 by a second castle that included a stone tower with a surrounding bailey.

Once a formidable and intimidating place, it is now a complete ruin and appears as if it has somehow sunken into the green mound on which it stands. The tower is now roofless, yet for some reason the air is chilly within the thick stone walls, even on a hot summer day, and as the visitor climbs down into the now underground level, they invariably feel uncomfortable and uneasy. Indeed, during the reign of Henry VIII, it was described as being one of the "most heinous, contagious and detestable places within the realm."

During the Middle Ages, Lydford Castle was used as a prison and as a court of law, being the administration office for the Royal Forest of Dartmoor, and also the Stannary Court, which had jurisdiction over the procedures for tin mining in Devon as well as over the behavior of the tin miners. During the English Civil War, the castle was used by the Royalists as a gaol for Parliamentary supporters and soldiers.

Oddly enough the castle's main spectral inhabitant is said to be the spirit of the Hanging Judge, the infamous Judge Jeffreys, but not in a form expected of such a man. Jeffreys held court in many Devonshire towns, and although legend suggests that he was at his cruellest at Lydford, there is a distinct lack of historical evidence to suggest that he ever visited the village. Having said that, the legend of his ghost is strong in these parts, even though he is bizarrely said to appear as a huge black pig, snuffling and snorting around the castle and village.

Another ghostly figure is also reported to exist in the dark, deep recesses of the castle dungeon. This is a terrifying apparition that takes the dark, misty shape of a tall man. In addition, and strangely much like the Tower of London, the ghostly figure of a bear has also been reported in the castle grounds. Apparently it has been seen walking around before disappearing through a stone archway and leaving an icy chill wherever it has been.

David Farrant, President of the British Psychic and Occult Society and better known for his 1970s investigations into the Highgate vampire, notes on his website:

> Members of the Society spent an all-night vigil inside the ruins at full moon and the results were, to say the least, intriguing. Perhaps most apparent from the onset of this vigil was the decidedly cold atmosphere in the old dungeons in the ruins; added to this the fact that a trained Alsatian dog 'froze' at the top of the wrought-iron staircase leading to the dungeons and barked repeatedly at something unseen below. When eventually carried down the stairs, it whined continually and cringed in a corner, ignoring all attempts to be pacified.

As well, he noted, "The next incident occurred at exactly ten minutes to three when a dark shape, resembling a 'large bear', was seen to materialize in an adjacent alcove and appeared to glide for several feet before promptly disappearing just below a stone archway leaving behind an intense atmosphere of evil and icy coldness."

TAUNTON CASTLE

Somerset

....

https://museumofsomerset.org.uk/taunton-castle

Dating from the twelfth century, Taunton Castle was founded by William Gifford, Bishop of Winchester to defend the town of Taunton in Somerset and although extensively reconstructed and extended in the thirteenth century and again in the sixteenth century, parts of the building are believed to date from its earlier period. It fell into ruin by 1600 but was repaired during the Civil War, although afterward in 1662 the keep was demolished with only the base remaining today. After the Civil War, the castle became the location for the Assize Courts and in 1874 was purchased by the Somerset Archaeological and Natural History Society as the location for a new museum. The building now houses the Museum of Somerset and the Somerset Military Museum and was designated a Grade I building in 1952.

Inevitably, such a castle would have a reputation of being haunted, and Taunton Castle does not disappoint in this regard. The Great Hall of the castle, where many of the trials were carried out, is subject to the sound of disembodied marching feet, as are the corridors. On the castle landing, a man in period dress and wig and carrying a sword and pistol has been seen, although his identity is unknown, while the castle has also seen various poltergeist activity as well as the ghost of a fair-haired woman in clothing matching the Civil War period. As well, a fiddler by the name of Tom is said to haunt a room in the castle although he is never seen, only heard playing his fiddle.

In August 2006 the television series *Most Haunted* visited the castle with hostess Yvette Fielding noting that the Hanging Judge George Jeffreys may well haunt the location and that he has been seen walking along the empty corridors of the castle. Interestingly, in 2009 a privy that may have been used by Judge Jeffreys was discovered in the castle during archaeological excavations that recorded a number of previously unknown features. It is believed the privy was built when the castle was used for the Bloody Assizes in 1685 following the Monmouth Rebellion, when Jeffreys sentenced 144 people to be hanged, drawn and quartered.

Many workers refuse to enter the Somerset Room on their own as they feel as if they are being watched. As well, the room is subject to cold spots and wild temperature changes and is reputed to be haunted by a poltergeist who moves stuff around. Barry Hewitson, who worked at the castle, noted:

> One particular incident that I recall occurred a few years ago when I was doing some painting in the Somerset room. I was on top of some steps and for some reason or other, the whole room went cold, extremely cold ,and the hairs went up on the back of my neck. I had to stop work and come down the stairs to regain my composure. I looked around and there was nothing obvious there, but clearly there was something that caused the temperature to drop suddenly. I'm not a nervous person and I don't even believe in ghosts, but there certainly have been times when I felt that I wasn't alone in the building.

Ghost hunter and historian Richard Felix noted that a castle custodian, while cleaning a glass case, once felt as if something grabbed him by the neck, but there was no reflection in the glass. When he turned around and there was no one there, he realized that it had felt like a rope tightening around his neck.

OKEHAMPTON CASTLE
Devon

....

www.english-heritage.org.uk/visit/places/okehampton-castle

Built between 1068 and 1086 by Baldwin de Brionne, who was appointed Sheriff of Devon by William the Conqueror following a revolt against the Norman rulers, Okehampton Castle is the largest castle ruin in Devon and one of the largest in the South West. It sits on the northern edge of Dartmoor overlooking a wooded valley and is mentioned in the Domesday Book.

The castle was later acquired by the Courtenay family who, over time, rebuilt the Norman fortress in about 1297. In 1539, however, Henry Courtenay was executed by Henry VIII for treason and the castle was abandoned with the stones scavenged by local people.

It is said to be haunted by the ghost of Lady Howard who is said to have murdered her four husbands. At midnight every night she has been seen traveling from Okehampton to Tavistock in the back of a carriage constructed from the bones of her victims and driven by a headless driver.

Kevin Hynes, in his book *Haunted Dartmoor*, recalls how he visited the castle in 2013 and spoke to a member of staff about hauntings and ghosts at the castle. The staff member apparently quite happily shared two incidences experienced by her colleagues, the first being the sighting of a large black dog in the grounds, which upon further inspection had simply disappeared, and the other, a brush with Lady Howard herself, seen at sunrise sitting naked next to the river brushing her hair.

Is it possible that a lack of visitors to this castle is directly proportional to the number of reported ghostly occurrences? I guess one will never know.

OLD WARDOUR CASTLE
Wiltshire
....

www.english-heritage.org.uk/visit/places/old-wardour-castle

Inspired by the hexagonal castles then in fashion in France, Old Wardour Castle in Wiltshire was constructed in the 1390s and later partially destroyed in 1643 and 1644 during the English Civil War. Designated a Grade I building, it was purchased in 1547 by Sir Thomas Arundell of Cornwall who married a sister of Catherine Howard, the fifth queen of Henry VIII. However, Sir Thomas soon became involved in treasonous activity and was later executed.

Arundell's great grandson, the 2nd Lord Arundell, was later killed fighting for King Charles in the Civil War and the castle was besieged. Lady Blanche Arundell and her soldiers then held out for six days against a determined enemy but eventually she surrendered and parliamentary troops took control of the castle.

The next heir, Henry, then led a counter siege, but the defending soldiers held out until gunpowder was accidentally set alight and a devastating explosion destroyed two towers and weakened the castle walls. Henry took advantage of this misfortune and managed to take back control. When the war ended and the Parliamentarians were victorious, the castle was seized. It was later returned to the family after the Monarchy was restored.

The castle was never rebuilt, but legend suggests that a number of restless spirits remain, with the ghost of Lady Blanche Arundell said to haunt the castle grounds.

Incidentally, Old Wardour Castle was used for filming parts of the movie *Robin Hood—Prince of Thieves* starring Kevin Costner and has also been used for numerous other television programs.

PENDENNIS CASTLE
Cornwall
····················

www.english-heritage.org.uk/visit/places/pendennis-castle

An artillery fort constructed between 1540 and 1542 by Henry VIII and standing near Falmouth in Cornwall, Pendennis Castle formed a strategic part of the defense of England against invasion from France and the Holy Roman Empire, as well as defended the mouth of the River Fal.

In 1646, the castle was held by Royalists and was only taken by Cromwell after a long siege. Indeed, it was the last royalist castle in England to fall to the Parliamentarians and then only because the defenders were suffering starvation. However, unlike most castles, Cromwell did not slight as he deemed it important in the defense of the country. Later concerns about a possible French invasion resulted in its defenses being modernized in the 1730s and again during the 1790s during the Napoleonic Wars, and in the 1880s and 1890s an electrically operated minefield was laid across the River Fal, as well as new rapid firing guns.

The castle also saw service during both the First and Second World Wars, but in 1956 it was deemed obsolete and decommissioned. Today it is managed by English Heritage as a tourist attraction and is considered "one of the finest examples of a post-medieval defensive promontory fort in the country."

Jane Rowe, Visitors Operations Manager notes, "perhaps it's not surprising that it's thought to be home to at least eight different ghosts, including a lieutenant governor, scullery girl, and head cook. All our haunted tales are based on sightings that have been reported time and again by different sources, and visitors are always eager to hear how they can be linked back to actual historical events and people."

The ghostly piercing screams of a kitchen maid who fell to her death while carrying a tray of food have been heard by numerous visitors, as have strange footsteps around the staircase area which are attributed to another ghostly presence, the spirit of head cook Maude. In the keep of the castle the ghost of an unknown woman has been heard humming and witnesses have reported feeling a shiver of fear when they have heard her. On one occasion, it was reported that a witness to an apparition told how he saw somebody standing at the bottom of the stairs in the keep which then spoke to him saying "I'm here on the wall".

As well, people have reported hearing the ghostly sound of horse's hooves thought to belong to ill-fated horses eaten by the defenders during the civil war siege of 1646. And scarily, visitors have often reported the sounds of children's laughter from empty rooms.

PENGERSICK CASTLE
Cornwall
....
www.pengersickcastle.com

Pengersick Castle has the unenviable reputation of being one of the most haunted locations in Cornwall. There is evidence that the site has been occupied as far back as the Bronze Age, although the Pengersick family have lived here since the twelfth Century. Ostensibly a fortified manor house, it is a Grade II building and was built in the early 1500s.

Pengersick, which means the "head of a marshy place," is built upon boggy ground, hence the name, and reports suggest that more than twenty separate ghosts haunt the castle and its grounds, the most common being the apparition of a monk who is often seen near a small forested area at the end of the medieval garden. Interestingly, he is said to wear a wide brimmed hat.

A number of guests have been alarmed by the appearance of a ghostly woman in the early hours of the morning in the main bedroom, who suddenly appears by the window, gazing forlornly out at the night sky before turning and walking slowly to a Jacobean four-poster bed where she lies down and clutches her stomach, writhing in apparent agony. Another female figure is also said to appear in the room and stands at the bedside. Investigators have suggested that the woman in pain may have been poisoned sometime in the past and the other woman is a maid, nursing her through her last painful hours. Ron Kirby, a douser, noted about the main bedroom: "When we first came here about four years ago we started to douse the bedroom and all together, we found twenty-eight presences spread out over a period of 300 years between 1500 and 1814, which is when the last one occured."

In 2003, historian and ghost hunter Richard Felix from the television series *Most Haunted* put forward the following theory regarding one of the ghosts that haunt the castle. "Now there's a story concerning the White Lady who wanders in the bedrooms; they believe it to be Engrina (Pengersick). But she didn't live here, she lived up the road when the house was up there. So I wondered why she would haunt this place and then, of course, I asked the question, did they use the same stone from that house to build this one. And they did. So there's every possibility that the ghost of Engrina is haunting the new house."

The ghost of a thirteen-year-old girl is also reported to haunt the battlements and is believed to attempt to push people over the side if she doesn't approve of them. It is suggested that she was blown over the edge by a strong gust of wind whilst dancing and her tormented spirit has never moved on. The ghost of a young boy has been known to go around pulling on women's dresses or attempting to hold their hands, as if searching for his mother.

Other eerie reports include a ghostly cat called Alexander, electrical equipment that inexplicably fails, orbs and other weird shapes that show up on some photographs, a devil-dog with fiery red eyes, and a creepy white mist that slowly drifts toward terrified witnesses.

POWDERHAM CASTLE
Devon
....
www.powderham.co.uk

Powderham Castle, the ancestral home of the Earl and Countess of Devon, was built in 1379 by Sir Phillip Courtenay, and is one of the oldest family homes in England. Although called a castle, it is actually a fortified manor house and is situated on flat, formerly marshy ground on the west bank of the River Exe estuary in Devon, about 10 kilometers south of Exeter. It is a Grade I building.

During the Civil War, the castle was garrisoned by three hundred Royalist soldiers and in December 1645, a Parliamentarian detachment under the command of Sir Thomas Fairfax tried to capture it.

The castle however, remained strong but later fell in January 1646. During the sieges, the castle was badly damaged and remained that way until the early 1700s when it was repaired by Sir William Courtenay.

Around two hundred years ago, during renovation work to the Guard Tower, one of castles oldest sections, it was discovered that an ancient wall was hollow and, upon breaking the wall down, workmen were horrified to discover a room that contained the bones of a woman and a baby. The remains were quickly reinterred in nearby Powderham Church, but it seems that this did little to quell the restless spirits and, according to several mediums, they were bricked up alive and left to die. The woman's ghostly apparition is frequently seen holding her child as she moves around the castle in a state of abject despair.

Another ghostly figure that roams the castle is that of the Grey Lady, who has been witnessed on numerous occasions, either walking slowly between the castle and Powderham Church, or else appearing in the library where she leaves a cold chill in her spectral wake. She is believed to be Lady Frances, who married Viscount Courtenay in 1741, and although a seemingly benign ghost, it is said that a visit from her spirit is a bad omen and foreshadows the death of the head of the house.

ST BRIAVELS CASTLE
Gloucestershire

···················

www.english-heritage.org.uk/visit/places/st-briavels-castle

A moated Norman castle in Gloucestershire, St Briavels Castle was originally built between 1075 and 1129 as a royal administrative center for the Forest of Dean. It is noted for its enormous Edwardian gatehouse that sits at the entrance to the castle, as well as being the favorite hunting lodge of King John during the thirteenth century. It later became a major manufacturing center in England for the making of quarrels which were required for crossbows.

It was subsequently used as a court and a debtor's prison, although following local riots and a parliamentary investigation in the 1830s, it was shut down as a prison due to its inhumane conditions. Given the conditions in gaols in the 1800s, one can only imagine how terrible it was for it to be closed down.

In 1948 it was renovated and adapted to a youth hostel, which it remains to this day. It is classed as a Grade I building and as a Scheduled Monument and has the reputation as being one of the most haunted castles in England with very few visitors leaving without witnessing something of an unexplained nature. As such, it has become the number one hot spot for ghost hunters across the country.

Considerable poltergeist activity has been reported in the prison with voices and footsteps regularly heard and furniture being moved considerable distances. Others have reported the unpleasant sensation of being grabbed by unseen hands while some have reporting unnerving growling noises.

The castle keep area is believed to be haunted by a ghost in a full suit of armor who has been witnessed at night, the light of the moon glinting off his armor, while in the solar room the sound of a crying baby is often heard. Interestingly, during recent renovations to the room, the corpse of a baby wrapped in linen fell from the ceiling which led some to suspect that the baby was the source of the crying.

Dark figures have been seen in the Chaplain's Room, often standing in the doorway and seemingly blocking people's escape. As well, strange flashes of light and red orbs have been regularly seen and people have reported the sensation of being touched by invisible hands. And, similar to the prison area, furniture and beds have been known to move seemingly by themselves. Others have witnessed indentations on their beds as if someone is sitting down.

In the hanging room the appearance of a dark figure has been witnessed standing in the doorway and people have reported being violently pushed. Strange sounds have also been reported, including humming noises and something described as being similar to that of marbles dropping. In the constable's room, people report a putrid and nauseous rotting smell, doors that swing open, and feelings of light headedness and strangulation.

In the porters lodge a man staying at the castle reported the feeling of being pinned down on his bed by an unseen assailant while in the same area, a misty and sometimes dark shadow has been seen near the fireplace as well as the doorway. The sound of a crying child has also been reported as has a strange scraping sound that people have described as being like a body being dragged across the floor.

The oubliette is said to contain an angry spirit that tugs upon people's bed sheets, and some people have reported being awoken by a woman screaming while the state apartment, one of the oldest remaining parts of the castle, is subjected to disembodied footsteps and scratching and banging from within the walls. It is believed that these noises are caused by the ghost of a young girl dressed in white who has been seen at the end of the corridor. Indeed, one guest has witnessed this girl walk through a wall. A dark entity has also been seen walking across the room and people have reported disembodied voices seemingly arguing as well as the sound of violins playing.

SUDELEY CASTLE
Gloucestershire
....
www.sudeleycastle.co.uk

A Grade I private residence in the Cotswolds in Gloucestershire, Sudeley Castle was built in the fifteenth century, possibly on the site of a previous twelfth-century castle. It was where Catherine Parr, the sixth wife of King Henry VIII died from childbirth complications in September 1548

and her funeral was the first royal Protestant burial held in the country.

During the Civil War the 6th Lord Chandos of Sudeley allied himself with the Royalists and Charles I himself stayed here after his failed attempt to take Gloucester. The castle was taken briefly by Parliamentary forces who plundered the place, however, it was retaken by the Royalists before once again being taken by Parliament in 1644 after a concerted attack. It was then slighted in 1649.

Catherine Parr's ghost is said to wander the corridors of the castle and there have been numerous reports of a tall lady in a green dress seen around the castle nursery. Her appearances are often foretold by the faint smell of apple scented perfume and occasionally accompanied by the sobs of a crying child. Some staff members have claimed to have seen a melancholy figure looking out from a landing window that overlooks the gardens. Her ghost has also been seen in the Queen's Garden, again described as a melancholy figure who gazes forlornly into the ornate pond.

In another sighting, Margaret Parker, a maid who worked at the castle, reported seeing a tall, beautiful woman in a long green dress looking out of a window. She mistook the woman for an artist who was working in the castle on that particular day. However, as she was to soon find out, the artist was in a different part of the house and nowhere near the window where the woman was sighted. She noted, "Must be about nine years ago, it was the middle of winter (and) the castle was all locked up and it was just five girls and myself cleaning."

Interestingly, Catherine's ghost is also said to haunt Snape Castle in North Yorkshire, but as a carefree young girl with long fair hair wearing a blue Tudor-style dress.

Another restless spirit that haunts the castle is that of a housekeeper named Janet who was employed from 1896. She has been described as a formidable Scottish lady and apparently took the virtues of her young housemaids very seriously, each night sitting at the top of the stairs leading to their bedrooms armed with a feather duster to fend off the amorous approaches of the young menservants. She is described as being dressed in a mop cap, white blouse and long faded pink and white skirt. Her face is said to be contorted into a frown of displeasure. To this day her ghost has been seen by staff and visitors at the top of those very same stairs and several people ascending the stairs have reported encounters with her. On one occasion a teenage girl who strayed from a tour group came face-to-face with the housekeeper on the upstairs landing. She became hysterical when the apparition began waving a feather duster at her.

Janet's ghost is not confined to patrolling the stairs. She has been seen several times in the needlework bedroom as well as leaving the main guest bedroom and also entering the Rupert room. And apart from the two female spirits, the ghost of a man with a hawk perched on his arm has been seen in the castle grounds. No one knows who he is but it is suspected that he was once a servant, possibly one who looked after the birds of prey.

The caretaker at Sudeley Castle, when asked in the 1995 television series *Castle Ghosts of England* whether he thought the castle was haunted, noted, "Yes I do, I get the general feeling as do members of staff and visitors that there's something there."

TIVERTON CASTLE
Devon

....

www.tivertoncastle.com

The ruined remains of a medieval castle, it is thought to have been built by Richard de Redvers, first Earl of Devon, during the reign of Henry I. The castle occupies a defensive position above the banks of the River Exe at Tiverton in Devon and was a Royalist stronghold during the Civil War. Parliamentarian troops laid siege to it using the culverin, the largest artillery piece in use at the time and capable of firing up to two thousand yards. Although terribly inaccurate, one shot was lucky enough to hit one of the chains holding up the castle's drawbridge during the siege and the castle was quickly overrun and dismantled to ensure that it had no military importance whatsoever.

Today the castle comprises ruined defensive perimeter walls, towers, and buildings from various periods, and parts were converted to a country house in the seventeenth century. It is reputed to be haunted by a number of ghosts, including that of a woman who was unfortunately killed in a playful game of hide and seek after her wedding when she hid in a large chest which locked itself, tragically trapping the woman.

Legend has it that as her friends searched throughout the castle to find somewhere to hide, the bride came across the large carved chest in the corner of a corridor. She quickly climbed inside quietly congratulating herself at finding such a splendid place to hide, however, as she lowered the lid she heard a fateful click, and, to her horror, she found herself trapped.

Sometime later the chest was opened, and the awful secret of the disappearing bride was revealed, the now yellowed wedding dress covering a curled-up skeleton. Now it is said that her sorrowful figure wanders silently through parts of the old castle and people have reported seeing a figure at the far end of a certain room or passing through a doorway or looking out of a window.

As well, Hugh Spencer wanted his daughter to marry Sir Charles Trevor, a wealthy man who was much older than his daughter Alice. The castle manager at the time was a young man named Maurice Fortescue, who was secretly in love with Alice. However, things were not to turn out right as one day Fortescue's dog damaged Sir Charles's hat and he drew his sword killing the dog. In a rage, Fortescue punched Trevor, knocking him down. Offended by the younger man's impetuosity, Sir Charles challenged him to a duel. Realizing that he would likely lose the duel, Maurice confessed his love to Alice. Surprisingly Alice replied, "Maurice Fortescue, if in the duel with this wicked man you fall, the heart of Alice Spencer dies with you."

And with this the two combatants met in the woods by the river, and predictably Sir Charles, a vastly experienced swordsman, quickly prevailed, wounding the younger man before throwing his body into the river. Alice, who had been watching the duel from a tower window, ran to the river bank and cast herself in, trying in vain to rescue the mortally wounded Maurice. Both drowned, and legend suggests that whenever the River Exe is in flood, the ghosts of Alice, Maurice, and his hound can be seen walking in the woods below the castle.

FOUR

EAST ENGLAND

BACONSTHORPE CASTLE
Norfolk

....

www.english-heritage.org.uk/visit/places
/baconsthorpe-castle

Now a ruined fortified manor house hidden in the rural countryside of Norfolk, Baconsthorpe castle was constructed from around 1460 to 1486 by John Heydon and Sir Henry Heydon. Originally built without a license to fortify, it later became fortified and much more elaborate as the family's fortunes grew. However, as wealthy as the family was, they were poor financial managers and Christopher Heydon, who died in 1579 accumulated large debts, forcing his son William to sell off parts of the estate. Still, even with this financial set back, the family continued to spend extravagantly of the castle and by the mid-seventeenth century they were forced to demolish much of the castle to pay off their debts.

Today the ruins consist of complete curtain walls that include the remains of towers, forming a largish square court. The remains of a three-story gatehouse with a two-story projection for the drawbridge are in the middle of the south wall and the remains of a two-story range are along the east wall. It is also freely accessible to the public and is designated as a Grade I building and a Scheduled Ancient Monument.

And like most castles, it appears to hold at least one otherworldly inhabitant as a number of visitors have reported hearing splashing like sounds on the moat and upon investigating have noticed ripples radiating outward across the dark surface. Looking up, they have reported seeing a ghostly sentry standing on the walls, lobbing stones into the water. Who he is, no one knows. And why he throws stones into the water is equally unknown. Perhaps he is just bored, after all, centuries of patrolling the same battlements could do that to someone, maybe even a ghost.

CASTLE RISING
Norfolk
....

www.english-heritage.org.uk/visit/places/castle-rising-castle

A ruined medieval fortification in Norfolk, Castle Rising was built around 1138 by William d'Aubigny II, who had recently become the Earl of Arundel. It was later passed on to William's descendants before being acquired by the Montalt family in 1243. The Montalts later sold the castle to Queen Isabella, the alleged murderer of Edward II, who lived there in exile from 1330. While there, she extended the castle buildings and entertained her son, Edward III, on numerous occasions. After she died in 1358, the castle was granted to Edward, the Black Prince, as a part of the Duchy of Cornwall.

During the fifteenth century, the castle fell into disrepair and by the middle of the sixteenth century it was derelict. However, in the nineteenth century Mary and Fulke Greville Howard inherited the property and the castle was restored and renovated.

Many visitors to the castle have reported sighting figures dressed as monks while others say they have been pushed or nudged by invisible hands. However, as interesting as these reports are, Richard Jones notes in his book *Haunted Castles of Britain and Ireland* that "the upper rooms are said to be haunted by the ghost of one of the castle's most notorious former residents—Queen Isabella, the 'She-wolf of France.'"

He also suggests that "the echoes of her last troubled years are still said to rebound through the corridors of the castle. Several visitors have been shocked by the sound of hysterical cackling around the top floor of the building. Residents in the nearby village have occasionally been disturbed by ghostly screams and maniacal laughter coming from the castle in the early hours of the morning."

Interestingly, in 2016 the Essex Ghost Hunting Team claimed that they had photographic evidence of Isabella's ghost when one of their members, known only as Andy, snapped a strange photograph recalling; "There were around seven of us in the room at the time. My friend turned to me and whispered, 'can you hear anything?' so I listened carefully, and it sounded just like the sound of a long dress swishing over the stones coming up the stairway outside. I decided to take a picture to see what I might capture and then realized that there was what appeared to be a figure standing in the middle of the room."

After looking at the photo on the computer he noted that there was "a clear figure that, from the clothing and the shoulder pads, looks like someone wearing medieval dress. They even look to have something on their head, like a queen might wear. But what is most striking is the fact there is a doglike shape at her feet."

COLCHESTER CASTLE

Essex

....

https://cimuseums.org.uk/visit/venues/colchester-castle

Built on the foundations of an earlier Roman temple, Colchester Castle was designed by Gundulf, Bishop of Rochester on the orders of William the Conqueror and building began between 1069 and 1076 under the supervision of Eudo Dapifer, who became the castles steward on its completion.

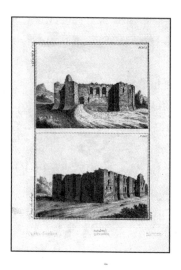

The construction work ceased in 1080 because of a threat of invasion, but the castle was completed by around 1100. In 1215, the castle was besieged and eventually captured by King John during the First Barons' War. In later years the castle was used as a county prison and in 1645 was used by the Witchfinder General, Matthew Hopkins to interrogate and imprison suspected witches. In 1648, during the Second English Civil War, Royalist leaders Sir Charles Lucas and Sir George Lisle were executed just to the rear of the castle. Local legend suggests that grass will not grow on the spot on which they fell and a small obelisk now marks the point.

Interestingly, the castle's keep is the largest ever built in Britain and the largest surviving example in Europe. It is a Grade I building.

The ghost of James Parnell, a Quaker, is said to haunt the castle. In 1656 he was arrested and imprisoned for blasphemy and other offenses. He was fined forty pounds by the magistrate, but he refused to pay and as such was returned to Colchester Castle. Due to the cruelty of his gaoler, he was forced to climb a rope to get his food. Parnell fell from the rope and was badly injured, finally dying from these injuries. His tortured ghost is said to roam the castle, his pained groans echoing in the corridors and walls of the castle. Local legend suggests that, many years ago, a man once stayed the night in the dungeons as a wager, only to emerge the next day a gibbering wreck.

Other stories concerning the castle involve sightings of Roman and Royalist soldiers walking around the grounds.

FRAMLINGHAM CASTLE
Suffolk
· · · · · · · · · · · · · · · · ·

www.english-heritage.org.uk/visit/places/framlingham-castle

Located in Suffolk, Framlingham Castle was originally a Norman motte-and-bailey castle built in 1148 and later destroyed by Henry II in the aftermath of the revolt of 1173.

Roger Bigod, the Earl of Norfolk, then built a new castle on the site but this was later taken by King John in 1216 after a short siege. Interestingly, the castle did not have a keep and relied instead upon a curtain wall with thirteen towers to defend the centre. However, by the end of the thirteenth century, the castle had become more of a hunting lodge utilizing its extensive parklands as hunting grounds.

Extensive gardens were built within the castle during the fifteenth and sixteenth centuries and older parts were redesigned to allow extensive views. Sadly, by the end of the sixteenth century, the castle fell into disrepair and in 1636 it was given to Pembroke College for use as a poor house, which it remained until 1839 when the facility closed. During the Second World War, it became a part of the regional defenses against German invasion and these days it is managed by English Heritage as a popular tourist attraction.

The castle, unsurprisingly, has a multitude of ghostly happenings from mysterious disembodied faces, ghostly footsteps and unearthly ghostly screams which have been reported by staff and visitors echoing through the castle's downstairs rooms. And, as recently as 2013, there were reports of children's voices coming from the empty courtyard with some suggesting that the voices sounded as if they were playing.

HADLEIGH CASTLE

Essex

·················

www.english-heritage.org.uk/visit/places/hadleigh-castle

Overlooking the Thames estuary from a ridge to the south of Hadleigh in Essex, Hadleigh Castle was built after 1215 by Hubert de Burgh during the reign of Henry III. It was later upgraded and significantly expanded by Edward III, who not only turned it into a grander property to defend against potential French attacks but to provide the King with suitable lodgings close to London.

Sadly, the castle was built on a hill and as such has often been subject to subsidence that, when combined with the subsequent removal of its stonework in the sixteenth century, has led to its now ruined state. The remains are now protected by English Heritage as a Grade I building and Scheduled Monument.

During the nineteenth century, it was rumored that smugglers used secret chambers in the ruins of the castle to hide their goods. They burned colored lights and made strange noises to frighten away nosy locals. Highwayman Dick Turpin was also reputed to have used the ruins with his gang.

It was around this time that the castle got its reputation for being haunted by a woman in white. A milkmaid called Sally, from nearby Castle Farm, saw a ghostly woman early one morning. The ghost commanded Sally to meet her again at the castle at midnight. However, she was too frightened to go. The next morning, however, she was accosted by the ghostly woman who was so annoyed that she had been disobeyed that she hit the milkmaid around the head almost dislocating her neck. After this, the ghost was known as "Wry-neck Sal". In 1917 it was reported that the ghost was seen by a group of men out partying. When one of them chased her with a stick, she disappeared

As well, people have reported various sightings at the castle including a huge black devil-dog with red eyes to hearing the muffled voice of a woman talking. It has also thas been reported that the ghost of a man in black haunts the castle and offers to buy souls in return for a song.

The footpath leading to the ruins has been the scene of disembodied voices and there are reports of a ghostly woman in grey as well as a boy in knee-high shorts and a transparent white horse that sometimes appears to shock witnesses. And, recalling the smugglers and their use of colored lights to warn away unwanted visitors, it is not surprising that odd colored lights that flit through the ruins at night are also reported.

KIMBOLTON CASTLE
Cambridgeshire
....
www.kimbolton.cambs.sch.uk/castle

A country house in Cambridgeshire, Kimbolton Castle was originally a medieval castle but later converted into a stately palace and was the family seat of the Dukes of Manchester, with the castle being bought by Sir Henry Montagu, later

1st Earl of Manchester, in 1615. His descendants owned the castle for 335 years until it was sold in 1950. Catherine of Aragon was sent here in April 1534 for refusing to give up her status or deny the validity of her marriage to Henry VIII. However, the fenland climate was seriously damaging to her health and she died here in January 1536. It now houses Kimbolton School, a coeducational independent day and boarding school.

The castle has been the subject of many ghost stories over more than 900 years, but none involving anyone more famous than Catherine of Aragon, who, following a divorce from Henry VIII, was sent to Kimbolton Castle where she lived, partly as prisoner, until her death. However, some say a part of her still remains at the castle, with a number of sightings of her on the grand stairs. As well, bizarrely, her head and shoulders have been seen gliding along the floor, the ghost apparently unaware of the changes to the original floor levels over time.

"Catherine of Aragon, people say, haunts the castle," said castle historian Nora Butler. "Some dukes wrote fanciful tales of Catherine of Aragon running up and down the stairs long after she died."

Another former inhabitant of the Castle, Sir John Popham, reputedly threw his baby child out of a castle window into the courtyard. It is said that the stone upon which the baby landed glows red annually on the anniversary of this event. A third ghostly legend of similar uncertain origin describes a female apparition that periodically walks across a field north-east of the castle.

NORWICH CASTLE
Norfolk

....

www.museums.norfolk.gov.uk/Visit_Us/Norwich_Castle

Founded in the aftermath of the Norman conquest, Norwich Castle is the only Norman stronghold in East Anglia. It was besieged on numerous occasions and even captured by Louis, the Dauphin, heir to the King of France.

After the military importance of the castle declined, the castle became a prison which it remained until 1887. In 1894 the Norwich Museum moved to the castle and has since operated in this capacity.

The most sighted ghost of the castle is of a woman wearing a black dress. She was first recorded 1820 by several prisoners who were reportedly scared half to death. She is thought to be wearing Victorian clothing and wanders around the art exhibition area of the museum, turning a corner and then vanishing. She has also been seen in the grounds of the castle and is believed to be the spirit of Martha Alden who lived at Attleborough with her husband who she murdered in 1807. She was hung in July of the same year and has haunted the castle ever since.

WOODCROFT CASTLE

Cambridgeshire

....

*http://helpston.net/wp-content/uploads/2015/06
/The-History-of-Woodcroft-Castle.pdf*

A moated medieval castle in the parish of Etton in Cambridgeshire, Woodcroft Castle was erected at the end of the thirteenth century. The west range and a circular corner tower survive, with a later wing adjoining to the northeast. It is a private Grade II building.

The castle was held by the Royalists under the command of Michael Hudson during the English Civil War and was successfully besieged and taken by Parliamentary forces in 1648. Hudson was captured and sent to London, however, he escaped and returned to Woodcroft to defend it. Later, with Parliamentary troops swarming over the castle,

Hudson was thrown from one of the parapets but managed to cling onto a stone gargoyle. To remove his grip, an enemy soldier severed his fingers and he fell into the moat before swimming away. He was again captured and this time killed by a musket blow to the head before his tongue was cut off.

Hudson's ghost is said to haunt Woodcroft Castle today. Sometimes you can hear him shouting or begging for mercy or screaming. It is said that he is often seen around the time of his death, reenacting his fall into the moat.

FIVE

EAST MIDLANDS

BARNWELL CASTLE

Northamptonshire

....

www.castleuk.net/castle_lists_midlands
/141/barnwellcastle.htm

Built in 1266 during the reign of King Henry III by the powerful Berengar Le Moine family, the castle has huge thick walls some ten metres high and is situated south of the town, west of the village of Barnwell, in Northamptonshire. It is a Grade I building and a Scheduled Ancient Monument and sits on the site of a previous motte-and-bailey castle.

During the English Civil War it was used as an arsenal for the Royalists by its owner Sir Edward Montagu. Although in ruins, substantial parts of the castle remain and it is privately owned. Local legend suggests that the body of Berengar's brother, Wintner, is bricked up somewhere within its imposing walls.

The castle is supposedly haunted by the spectre of a woman prisoner by the name of Marie Le Maine who is said to have been bricked up alive soon after the castle was built. Her ghost has been witnessed by a postman, passing pedestrians and even a policeman who happened to be patrolling by the castle. As well, strong gusts of wind felt on windless days are attributed to the ghost of a murdered monk who is rumored to walk the grounds wielding a whip.

BOLSOVER CASTLE
Derbyshire
....
www.english-heritage.org.uk/visit/places/bolsover-castle

Built in the early seventeenth century by the Cavendish family on the site of a medieval castle founded in the twelfth century by the Peverel family, Bolsover Castle is a Grade I building. By the 1770s the castle was in a ruinous state and the estate passed to the Dukes of Portland, who kept the castle as a retreat until the early nineteenth century. For most of the nineteenth century it was tenanted and used as a vicarage. In 1946 it was passed over to the Ministry of Works, who stabilized and restored the buildings.

It is reportedly one of the most haunted sites in the region with staff and visitors alike having reported being pushed, seeing apparitions and items being moved as if by invisible hands. Some security guards have resigned after being spooked by seeing lights moving in parts of the property that were empty and hearing unexplained noises while on duty at night. On one occasion, it was reported that four builders working in the garden reported seeing a woman in a bustle-style dress who appeared and then subsequently disappeared though a wall. Two of the group declined to return the following day.

Diane Hinchcliffe, the site supervisor stated that; "Pretty much all the staff have had some experiences," although she noted that; "I am not necessarily a believer in ghosts. I think there is a rational explanation for everything, but there have been events that I cannot explain."

Display figures have moved around the site at night, whilst items left in a locked storeroom, including visitor's belongings, have also been moved although Hinchcliffe suggests that there is "the possibility of pranks and send ups." However, she also suggested that "there have been times when I have been the last to leave at night and the first to arrive in the morning and things have been changed. I have had things moved in locked rooms."

Visitors regularly report seeing ghostly figures. One of the most commonly sighted is said to be an apparition of a child, which is said to be seen holding the hands of young visitors. Ghostly figures have also been reported in the chamber under the castle, including a man wearing a ruff and a woman in a scarf who have been spotted standing together before vanishing. A ghostly woman has also been seen in the kitchen area ominously placing a small child into the fireplace before vanishing.

Why she is placing a child into the fireplace is unknown but the very thought of it conjures up horrific images.

LINCOLN CASTLE
Lincolnshire
....
www.lincolncastle.com

One of the most impressive Norman castles in the United Kingdom and built in 1068 on the site of a pre-existing Roman fortress, Lincoln Castle was one of the first motte-and-bailey castles to be constructed in England by William the Conqueror. The castle is unusual in that it has two mottes making it only one of two such castles in the country, the other example of this construction being at Lewes in Sussex.

On one of these mottes stands a fourteenth-century observatory tower whilst a twelfth-century shell keep, called Lucy Tower, sits atop the other. The castle also boasts two gates, a large round tower, and a cobb hall. Later additions included a prison, which has since been closed, and a Victorian courthouse which is still in use today. The castle also houses one of only four surviving copies of the Magna Carta. And with such an illustrious past, it is no wonder it is believed to be haunted.

Executions took place at the castle after it became a prison and this could help explain the amount of supernatural activity that is regularly reported throughout the castle, including frequent sightings of a lady carrying a baby who is seen walking down the stairs of the Old Victorian Women's Prison and unexplained lights inside the chapel where the doors have a habit of opening and closing by themselves. At the male prison, doors have been reported to slam shut and visitors have been shocked by the sound of keys jangling, footsteps and disembodied moans and screams.

Cobb Hall also has its ghostly apparitions with reports of a lady dressed in black who walks up and down the stairs leading to the old gallows, while the Observatory Tower is plagued by strange shadows and dark shapes descending the stairs. As well, visitors often report strange growls and crying in the prisoner's graveyard. A malnourished hound, once owned by a criminal who was hanged at the castle, spent the rest of its life waiting for its dead master and is now occasionally spotted around the castle walls still waiting.

In April 2004 Richard Hart and his partner Angela Allen got the fright of their lives when they took their two children up the observatory tower's stone stairs. Climbing the stairs they both experienced a chilling feeling. Hart used his digital camera to take some photographs and later, when he downloaded the pictures he found a ghostly image on one of the shots.

Hart noted that "All of a sudden, my partner started feeling really edgy and said she couldn't go up any further. I followed the children and although it was quite a warm day, I started to feel cold. When we went back down, there were some people looking after Angela and thinking she had suffered a funny turn. Angela is into the whole spiritual thing and we have heard before that she could be psychic so we wonder if she sensed something."

He also noted that none of the photos taken before or after showed the ghostly figure. "There really is no explaining it at all. It was really scary I have to say. I won't be going there again in a hurry."

Margaret Green, who runs the Lincoln Ghost Walk, stated that it was not the first time she had heard of strange happenings in the observatory tower. "About six or seven years ago a couple told me they were heading up the stairs and they saw a couple walking in front of them. When they reached the top, the couple had vanished and there was nowhere they could have gone. Last year, a young woman said that as she was walking up the steps, she started experiencing unbearable pain and had to be helped by other visitors. On the way back down the pain got less and less until it vanished. She asked me if anyone had ever been murdered there because she felt as though that was what was happening to her. It is possible that there is something ghostly there."

NEWARK CASTLE
Nottinghamshire
....
www.newark-sherwooddc.gov.uk/newarkcastle

Newark Castle, in Nottinghamshire, was originally a timber castle but was rebuilt in stone in the mid-twelfth century by Alexander, Bishop of Lincoln. In 1648 it was slighted after the English Civil War but was later restored by architect Anthony Salvin between 1845 and 1848. Further restoration works were carried out in 1889 and today it is a Scheduled Ancient Monument and a Grade I building as well as being recognized as an internationally important structure.

Interestingly, King John, the youngest of five sons of King Henry II and Eleanor of Aquitaine, died from dysentery after a feast at the castle in October 1216. On the night of his death a thunderstorm swept over the area and was later described in its ferocity as "the Devil himself coming to claim King John's soul".

It has been suggested that, in the early 1900s a castle ranger was found hanged in the King's Bedroom and tour guides have since reported seeing his ghost hanging from the ceiling, twitching and jolting as if struggling for breath. In the dungeon, voices and chanting have been heard while in the oubliette, a terrifying and oppressive place, visitors have reported a sense of unease as if they are being watched.

Strange unexplained flashes of light have been spotted in the castle grounds, as well as screaming and shouting being heard from the curtain wall which borders the river. Visitors in the castle grounds have also experienced cold spots and the undercroft is said to have a presence that sends cold shivers down your spine.

Peter Cox, who visited Newark Castle as a boy on a school trip, reported that he had a supernatural encounter one cold day in October when he went on a guided tour of the castle while on a school excursion. He explained that, in those days they got to see a lot more of the castle and had the opportunity of climbing down a ladder into the dungeon. He recalled that the temperature dropped rapidly and that the group was down there for at least ten minutes when he noticed something strange. "I could hear voices, not from the tour guide, they were hushed and almost muted. They grew louder and louder, and I remember asking my mate if he could hear anything. He said I was mad, but I'm sure that I could see someone in the corner, standing in the shadows watching us. I did no more and got back up the ladder to the opening as fast as I could."

And more recently, in 2015, Mr Lenny Low claimed to have taken a photograph showing the ghost of a fisher-woman while visiting the castle one overcast afternoon.

"When looking at the photos, one has a strange dark blemish in the right hand corner. Zoom in and this character appears, walking into what would be the pantry storeroom of the castle. It looks like how the fisherwomen of old dressed. The doorway it's walking into is fenced off but was the store-room of the castle, the kitchen is next door on the left. It looks like a woman with her sleeves rolled up in a busy like manner. Being 100 yards from the sea it's more likely to be a fisherman's wife—one who spent her time gutting and salting the fish."

NOTTINGHAM CASTLE
Nottinghamshire
....
www.nottinghamcastle.org.uk

Located on a natural outcrop known as Castle Rock, with cliffs 40 metres high to the south and west, Nottingham Castle holds a commanding position over the city. First constructed as a Norman motte-and-bailey in 1067, it was extensively rebuilt in stone by King Henry II from 1150. In 1194 it was being sieged by Richard the Lionheart as part of the campaign to put down the rebellion of Prince John. The Castle surrendered after just a few days.

In 1642 at the start of the Civil War, Charles I chose Nottingham as the rallying point for his armies, but soon after he departed, the castle was held by the Parliamentarians who repulsed several Royalist attacks. Then, in 1651, on the orders of John Hutchinson, the remnants of the castle were demolished. The Duke of Newcastle later built a mansion on the site; however, this was burnt down by rioters in 1831. The mansion was later rebuilt to house an art gallery and museum and these remain today, although very little of the original castle survives.

Nottingham Castle is said to be haunted by a number of different ghosts, with the main one being that of Roger Mortimer the Earl of March and lover of Queen Isobel, and who was probably her accomplice in the murder of Edward II. Sir Roger was imprisoned in the castle and later taken to London where he was hanged, drawn and quartered in November 1330. Under the castle, carved into the sandstone outcrop on which the castle stands, is a cave known as

Mortimer's Hole where Sir Roger Mortimer's ghost makes its presence known on occasions. His ghost is also heard pacing about his former cell as if unaware that he has been dead for centuries.

Equally, Queen Isabella's spirit is said to haunt the interior of the castle, screaming for her lost love while an unknown phantom child also lurks within the walls, appearing to shock visitors on occasions. Although it is unknown, it is possible that this ghostly child is one of the 28 sons of Welsh nobility that King John took hostage in 1212. The boys, some as young as 12, lived at the castle for some time, but were treated well and were allowed free rein within the walls. However, one day this all changed when John had them all executed in cold blood, taken up to the ramparts and hanged. It is said that the boy's pitiful cries for mercy still ring out around the castle.

PEVERIL CASTLE
Derbyshire

....

www.english-heritage.org.uk/visit/places/peveril-castle

Peveril Castle is a Scheduled Monument and a Grade I listed building overlooking the village of Castleton in the English county of Derbyshire. Also known as Castleton Castle or Peak Castle, it was built in the eleventh century as the main settlement of the feudal barony of William Peveril. It is mentioned in the Domesday Survey of 1086.

William Peveril the Younger later inherited the castle, however, in 1155 it, as well as the Peveril estate, was confiscated by King Henry II. In 1199 William de Ferrers acquired the castle although it remained under royal control. The closest Peveril Castle came to seeing actual warfare was in 1216.

In 1223 the castle was returned to the Crown and by the end of the fourteenth century, the barony was granted to John of Gaunt, Duke of Lancaster. Having little use for the castle, he ordered its material to be stripped for re-use and the castle began to fall into disrepair. By 1609 it was a ruin and abandoned.

The ghost of a knight has been observed standing by the keep while his riderless horse trots around nearby, and strange banging and clanking has been reported after dark, with searches revealing no apparent source. As well, the ghost of an old lady and a phantom horse have been reported in the area.

TATTERSHALL CASTLE

Lincolnshire

....

www.nationaltrust.org.uk/tattershall-castle

Originally a stone castle or a fortified manor house, built by Robert de Tattershall in 1231, Tattershall Castle was largely rebuilt in brick and expanded by Ralph, 3rd Lord Cromwell, between 1430 and 1450. Today it remains one of the three most important surviving brick castles of the mid-fifteenth century as brick castles were far less common in England than stone or earth and timber constructions as brick was chosen more often than not for its aesthetic qualities over defensive. About 700,000 bricks were used to build the castle, which has been described as the finest piece of medieval brick work in England.

Cromwell died in 1456 with the castle inherited by his niece, Joan Bouchier. However, it was soon confiscated by the Crown only to be recovered in 1560 by Sir Henry Sidney, who later sold it to Lord Clinton, later the Earl of Lincoln, where it remained until 1693. After this it was passed to the Fortesques before falling into disrepair. Today it is managed by English Heritage and is open to the public.

Although seemingly quiet with regards to the supernatural, the castle is nevertheless said to be haunted by the ghost of a White Lady who walks the lonely battlements at night. Who she is, no one knows.

Although I have not visited Tattershall castle since I was a young boy in the 1970s, I still remember the feelings of awe, wonderment and, somewhat, apprehension. From its majestic red turrets one could watch F4 Phantom jets as they landed and took off at a nearby RAF base, which was truly exciting as a young boy. And yet, it is that feeling of something else that remains with me to this day. That indescribable feeling that I was not alone in this place …

SIX

⤶

WEST MIDLANDS

ACTON BURNELL CASTLE

Shropshire

·················

www.english-heritage.org.uk/visit/places
/acton-burnell-castle

A thirteenth-century fortified manor house located in Shropshire, Acton Burnell Castle is a Grade I listed building. It is thought that the first Parliament of England where the Commons were fully represented was held here in 1283.

In 1284, Robert Burnell obtained a license to crenelate from the king although, given the large size of the first-floor windows of the castle, it would appear that it was designed to impress rather than have any serious defensive aspirations.

Abandoned by 1420, it was allowed to decay while a new house, Acton Burnell Hall was built next to it in the eighteenth century and all that remains today are the impressive ruins of the outer shell of the manor house and the gable ends of the barn.

The castle has long been rumored to be haunted by a girl in a white dress and in February 2004, student Stuart Edmunds and a group of friends visited Acton Burnell Castle after dark and came away with the impression that the ghost was very real. Edmunds was quoted as saying to the online BBC that:

> As I walked towards a doorway in the darkness, there appeared to be the silhouette of a figure in the doorway. As I stood frozen on the spot my immediate explanation was that someone had seen our torch light and come to throw us off the grounds. But as I stood alone in silence, I heard a breath above the sound of my own breathing. To hear more clearly, I held my breath and to my astonishment the dark shadow moved toward me. Without thinking I took a photo in the direction of the figure and saw in the flash light the misty face of a young woman and a portion of her white lace dress floating upward. I managed to get this photo which shows a mist towards the wall and a distorted face.

ASTLEY CASTLE

Warwickshire

....

www.arburyestate.co.uk/index.php?page=astley-castle

Now a modern holiday home, Astley Castle was previously a ruined, fortified sixteenth-century manor house as well as a Grade II listed building and a Scheduled Ancient Monument. It belonged to the Astley family from the twelfth century but passed to the Greys in 1420 when Joan de Astley, wife of Reginald Grey, 3rd Baron Grey de Ruthyn, inherited the estate. It is believed that the Greys rebuilt the manor house around 1555. After the Greys were disgraced, it passed to the monarchy and later, during the English Civil War, it was garrisoned by Parliament. In the 1960s it became a hotel, but this was short lived and the building was severely damaged by fire in 1978. It is believed that Lady Jane Grey may haunt its rooms and corridors.

Henry Grey, Duke of Suffolk, was the father of Lady Jane Grey. He was beheaded on 23 February 1554 after being convicted of high treason for his part in Sir Thomas Wyatt's attempt to overthrow Queen Mary after she announced her intention to marry Philip II of Spain. Henry's headless ghost is also said to haunt the castle.

Interestingly, following the fire of 1978, Gef White, a journalist for the *Tribune*, wrote, "The mystery is intriguing investigators of the blaze. A room was exposed by the fire and detectives were shown a circle of black lace, horror masks and three 'death ritual' dolls, stabbed by nails coated in red paint. The room, tucked away in a top corner of the castle, contained three dolls. The faces of each were painted in a tragic grimace and nails pierced their hearts and legs. On the door of the room was a hand-painted symbol like a huge question mark."

Maybe Astley Castle holds more secrets than we know.

DUDLEY CASTLE
Warwickshire
....

www.dudleyzoo.org.uk/dudley-castle

DUDLEY CASTLE KEEP. S.J.99.

According to legend, a Saxon Lord by the name of Dud constructed a wooden castle on the site where Dudley Castle stands today. Although this claim is not taken seriously by historians, it is thought that Ansculf de Picquigny built the first structure, a wooden motte-and-bailey, in 1070 and that his son, William Fitz-Ansculf, was in possession of the castle when it was recorded in the Domesday Book of 1086.

During the English Civil War in the 1640s the castle was garrisoned by Royalist troops and was twice laid under siege, the first being in 1644. With the tide of war going against the Royalists, a Parliamentarian General, Sir William Brereton, advanced toward Dudley for the second siege after which Colonel Leveson, commander of the Royalist garrison, surrendered the castle on the 13th of May 1646.

As with most Royalist garrisons, the castle was destroyed, and all of its defenses demolished. The keep, gatehouse, and defensive walls were all ruined although the domestic buildings were surprisingly spared. However, in 1750 a fire swept through the remains and, as it was rumored that the local militia kept their gunpowder in the castle, nothing was done to put out the fire. Dudley Castle was reduced to a romantic ruin.

It is now regarded as one of the most haunted locations in the Midlands and perhaps the British Isles themselves. There are many spirits that have been reported here throughout hundreds of years, although the most famous of these is that of the Grey Lady, believed to be the spirit of Dorothy Beaumont who lived in the castle for a time and gave birth to a daughter there. Sadly, the daughter died during birth, and various complications led to Dorothy's death soon after.

Dorothy apparently asked to be buried beside her daughter and expected that her husband would attend the funeral. However, neither of these happened and as a result, she continues to be tormented to this day and is said to wander aimlessly around the castle and its grounds.

Her ghost has often been seen near the castle keep as well as in the Grey Lady Tavern, a pub on the castle grounds that was named after her. Since opening, there have been reports of a strange blue mist that floats through the bar and is often accompanied by unexplained sounds. As well, the pub experiences alarms going off and extreme drops in temperature.

In August 2014 a couple, Dean and Amy Harper, managed to take a photograph of what appeared to be the famous Grey Lady and a young child in the door of Sharington Range, a set of buildings within the castle. Speaking to the *Birmingham Mail*, Dean Harper stated that "we went up to the castle ruins and while we were up there we thought we'd get some pictures of the grounds. On looking through the images that night, Amy saw a glow, as though a light was on on the top window level. On zooming in we noticed on the bottom, inside an arch, there was a lady and what appears to be a little girl, too."

About a year after the photograph came to light, another shot was taken by Lee Machin, apparently capturing the image of a shadowy figure in virtually the same spot. Machin, who was visiting the zoo enclosed within the castle walls, was taking a photo of his nine-year-old nephew and, when later looking through the images, noticed a startling sight—an indistinct ghostly figure standing in an archway.

Another frequently seen ghost at the castle is that of a Civil War drummer boy. He was reputedly killed by a bullet from a musket and he's been heard numerous times at night, tapping out various drum rolls as if in battle. Legend has it that it's deemed bad luck to hear or see him.

Apart from this, the most haunted location in the castle is thought to be the chapel undercroft, and in one room there is a stone coffin that is believed to have held the body of John Somery, apparently one of the castle's most feared lords. People have reported seeing disembodied legs beside the coffin while others have reported having their clothes tugged and their bodies prodded. Others have also reported strange grinding noises coming from the chapel above which, upon investigation, abruptly stop.

GOODRICH CASTLE

Herefordshire

....

www.english-heritage.org.uk/visit/places/goodrich-castle

Originally an earth-and-wooden fortification, probably built by Godric of Mappestone after the Norman invasion, Goodrich Castle was replaced with a stone keep in the middle of the twelfth century and was later expanded again during the late thirteenth century. It was the seat of the Talbot family before they fell out of favour in late Tudor times.

At the end of the eighteenth century it became a noted picturesque ruin and the subject of many paintings and poems, and even provided the inspiration for Wordsworth's 1798 poem *We are Seven*. Today it is a pretty ruin standing on a wooded, rocky spur overlooking the tranquil waters of the River Wye and is open to the public.

It is said that during the English Civil War siege, Alice Birch, the niece of a Parliamentarian officer, took refuge in the castle with her Royalist lover, Charles Clifford, a young officer. When it became clear that the fortress could no longer stand up to the constant bombardment, Clifford and Birch mounted a horse and, under cover of darkness, rode from the castle, managing to break through the enemy lines.

Sadly, heavy rains had swollen the River Wye and its muddy banks were slippery and dangerous. Attempting to cross the raging waters the horse lost its footing and the two lovers were swept away to their untimely deaths. Their ghosts, mounted on horseback, have been seen in the grounds of the castle as well as struggling in the river. Passersby have also reported seeing the ghosts staring from the ruined ramparts late at night.

As well, the Great Keep, sometimes called the "Macbeth Tower," is reputed to be haunted by the ghost of an Irish chieftain who was held prisoner there. Legend suggests that he died attempting to escape, which is why his ghost is said to still haunt the Tower

HOPTON CASTLE
Shropshire
·················
www.hoptoncastle.org.uk

Situated in Shropshire, Hopton Castle was probably founded in the twelfth century as a motte-and-bailey and later rebuilt in stone by Walter de Hopton during the Barons' War of the 1260s. During the English Civil War it was owned by Sir Henry Wallop. He fortified it as a parliamentary stronghold at the outbreak of the war but died before he could take part in the conflict, leaving it to his son, Robert Wallop,

The castle was apparently still habitable in 1700 but fell into disrepair soon afterward although substantial remnants of the keep remain. In 2010 it featured in the British TV series *Time Team* and was officially reopened to the public as a visitor attraction in December 2011 by the Duke of Gloucester. Now a romantic ruin, it is reputed to be haunted by a group of Parliamentarian soldiers who met their untimely end in the icy waters of the castle moat.

During the Civil War, it was one of the few castles in the west to be held by Parliament. In 1644 Royalist troops numbering around five hundred laid siege to the castle which was defended by about thirty Roundheads under the command of Samuel More. More, overwhelmingly outnumbered, eventually agreed to surrender.

Accounts vary as to what happened after the surrender, however, the surrendered Parliamentarian troops were massacred and then thrown into the moat. As a result, the castle is said to be haunted by the ghosts of the murdered men as well as four Royalist soldiers who died in the fighting. The ghost of Elizabeth Mayrick, the widow of one of the men, is also said to haunt the castle, crying for her lost love.

KENILWORTH CASTLE
Warwickshire

······················

www.english-heritage.org.uk/visit/places/kenilworth-castle

Built over several centuries and founded in the 1120s around a commanding Norman tower constructed by Geoffrey de Clinton, Kenilworth Castle was significantly renovated and enlarged by King John at the beginning of the thirteenth century, turning it into one of Britain's most impressive castles.

In 1266, the castle was the subject to the six-month long Siege of Kenilworth, which is believed to have been the longest siege in English history and formed the base for Lancastrian operations during the Wars of the Roses. As well, it was also the scene of the removal of Edward II from the English throne and the French insult to Henry V in 1414.

John of Gaunt, son of Edward III, spent lavishly and eventually developed the castle into a palace, constructing the great hall and associated rooms. In 1563, Elizabeth I bestowed the palace to Robert Dudley, the Earl of Leicester.

In 1649, the castle was partly destroyed by Parliamentary forces to ensure that it could no longer be used as a Royalist stronghold, and during the eighteenth century it became somewhat of a tourist destination and these days is managed by English Heritage.

It is a Grade I listed building and as a Scheduled Monument, it is open to the public.

It is said that it is haunted by a number of ghosts from different periods in the castle's history, including a man dressed in black who was killed in a sword fight at the castle gatehouse and a ghostly boy who has been regularly seen in the castle stables, surprisingly, along with ghostly horses and chickens.

Apart from this, the gatehouse is said to be haunted by the spirit of an old woman and a little girl who is said to appear to visitors and ask them where her father is.

LUDLOW CASTLE
Shropshire

....

www.ludlowcastle.com

Ludlow Castle is a now-ruined medieval fortress sitting on a rocky outcrop overlooking the River Teme. It was probably founded by Walter de Lacy after the Norman Conquest and was one of the first stone castles to be built in England, consisting of a rectangular outer bailey and an oval inner bailey entered through a gatehouse called the Great Tower which was installed during the Civil War when the castle changed hands several times. Sadly, after the Civil War, the castle became neglected and quickly fell into ruin.

The castle is reputed to be haunted by Marion de la Bruere who, roughly nine hundred years ago, had a secret lover called Arnold de Lys who got into the castle by a rope that Marion lowered over the battlements. However, one night de Lys betrayed her by leaving the rope available to his soldiers who then entered the castle and began killing the occupants. Realizing that she had been tricked, the despairing Marion leapt out of bed, grabbed de Lys' sword and killed him after which she leapt to her death from the top of the Pendover Tower, also known as the hanging tower.

It has been reported that Marion's ghost can sometimes be seen at dusk wandering around the base of the tower itself and that her screams can be heard on the anniversary of her death. The Hanging Tower is also supposed to be haunted by the sound of heavy breathing, attributed to a ghostly soldier, while many visitors and staff have reported hearing voices from empty rooms as if someone is having a conversation.

TAMWORTH CASTLE
Staffordshire
....
www.tamworthcastle.co.uk

A Grade I listed building, Tamworth Castle is a Norman castle located in Staffordshire. Overlooking the River Tame, the site has been inhabited since Anglo-Saxon times, and today it is one of the best-preserved Norman motte-and-bailey castles in England.

TAMWORTH CASTLE COURTYARD, 8.J.98

Built mainly in the late twelfth century, the castle was first constructed in 913 AD by Alfred the Great's daughter then later, William the Conqueror, who gave the land to Robert De Marmion who built the keep and curtain walls that stand to this very day. Unlike many castles however, it somehow escaped being destroyed by Oliver Cromwell during the English Civil War.

It is, of course, rumored to be haunted by a number of spirits, so much so that the middle chamber of the Norman tower is called 'the ghost room' for fairly obvious reasons given that the apparition of the "Black Lady of Tamworth" has been sighted on numerous occasions. The Black Lady is allegedly the ghost of a nun named Editha who founded an order in the ninth century and who were ejected from their convent by Robert de Marmion. Despairing for their future the nuns prayed to their founder and, as legend has it, she appeared at a banquet one night and attacked Marmion, warning him that unless the nuns could return to their convent, he would succumb to a terrible and painful death. She then struck him on the side with the point of her crosier, and the wound from the blow was so terrible that Marmion's agonising cries awoke the whole castle. The pain only ceased when he vowed to allow the nuns to return.

Apart from the Black Lady of Tamworth and her interesting, if slightly unbelievable, exploits from the grave, many have claimed to have seen another apparition, this time known as the White Lady. She is said to have been kidnapped and imprisoned in the tower by an evil knight by the name of Sir Tarquin, and despite his evil intents, she fell in love with him until, one day, Sir Lancelot du Lac decided to rescue her, slaying Tarquin in the process. The White Lady was so distraught that she threw herself from the battlements, and her ghost is now seen walking the battlements and crying mournfully.

Other ghostly encounters at the castle include a member of staff who was working in the Tamworth Story room when she felt as if someone had thrown sand into her eyes. At the very moment she felt this, a colleague reported seeing a blue mist swirl around the room. A visitor to the castle also reported an almost identical experience just outside a room known as the Haunted Bedroom. He reported that it felt as though somebody had thrown something in his eyes.

In another inexplicable encounter a member of staff was alone in the castle one night waiting in the reception area while a technician was outside checking the alarm system. She heard footsteps and furniture being moved about the room above her and, knowing that no one was in the room, fled outside where she met the alarm technician. When she explained what had happened he told her that he had seen a strange figure looking down at him from one of the windows.

TUTBURY CASTLE

Staffordshire

....

www.tutburycastle.com

Now largely ruined, Tutbury Castle in Staffordshire has stood since at least 1071 and was a popular destination for royalty. It was also the home of John of Gaunt, Second Duke of Lancaster, whose descendants included Henry IV, his son, Henry V, and his great grandson, Henry VI.

Over time the castle suffered from numerous sieges which resulted in the castle needing to be rebuilt, however, in 1647 Parliament ordered the castle to be destroyed after backing Charles I during the Civil War. By sheer good fortune, however, the castle wasn't completely destroyed, and the remains are now an elegant and picturesque ruin.

Importantly, Tutbury Castle is where Mary Queen of Scots was held captive on four separate occasions. And, as with many castles, ghosts are not unexpected visitors as it is believed to be haunted by Mary Queen of Scots, an apparition in a full suit of armor, a White Lady, a little boy, and a small girl.

Obviously the most famous of all these ghosts is Mary Queen of Scots. In 2004 she was witnessed standing at the top of the South Tower dressed in a full white Elizabethan gown peering down on a large group of visitors, apparently numbering upward of forty. When the group saw her, they thought it was a staff member and an elaborate ruse. However, it was later pointed out that no one on staff had a white gown and that they wouldn't have been in the tower anyway. Importantly, with this sighting, is that the whole group witnessed the phenomenon at the same time.

As well, people leaving the castle in their cars have reported seeing a figure dressed in black looking through the window of the Great Hall. This is also believed to be Mary, and one summer she was seen by several senior staff members who are generally reluctant to talk about anything supernatural. Apart from that, a team of archaeologists who were taking part in a dig at the castle, witnessed her as well.

As important an historical figure as Mary is, she is not the only ghostly figure that lurks within the ancient ruined walls as the ghostly figure of a man in a full suit of armor has been seen numerous times. He has been seen outside of John of Gaunt's Gateway, and on one occasion reportedly shouted, "Get thee hence!" He was last seen recently during the day by a visitor who reported hearing him say, "get over the fence," although there were no re-enactments scheduled for that day. Interestingly, one could surmise that the latter phrase was simply a misinterpretation of the former.

Recently, eerie footage of a shadowy figure standing motionless against a wall for almost twenty seconds before steadily moving across the room and out of sight was captured by a TV crew while filming at the castle. Minutes before the footage was taken, the crew had to stop filming because of a series of taps, footsteps, and bangs that came from apparently nowhere. Bex Palmer, codirector of *The Past Hunters*, then spotted the figure, noting; "It was so scary. I am quite tough on investigations, but I was terrified because it seemed as though it was coming towards us."

The figure, which has been previously reported, is said to be a man in a suit of armor known for shouting at guests and is locally known as "The Keeper."

Apart from the frightening knight and Mary Queen of Scots, a white human-shaped mist is often seen on the grassy bank around the North Tower, and a little boy wearing a white shirt has been seen sitting on the stairs of the great hall. He is so lifelike that many visitors assume he is real boy. The ghost of a girl called Ellie has often been sensed in the king's bedroom with visitors reporting her pulling fingers, holding hands, removing rings and causing an electric pulse in the arm.

In addition, film & TV crews often report batteries suddenly draining in their cameras and equipment. Strange blue lights have been witnessed moving around some of the rooms and at times they have been witnessed circling around people.

WARWICK CASTLE
Warwickshire
....
www.warwick-castle.com

Originally a wooden motte-and-bailey castle constructed on a bend of the River Avon, Warwick Castle was rebuilt in stone during the twelfth century and was used as a fortification until the early seventeenth century when Sir Fulke Greville converted it to a country house. The castle was taken in 1153 by Henry of Anjou, later King Henry II and later besieged in 1642 during the English Civil War. However, it survived and today is one of the most well-preserved medieval castles in England.

It is protected as a Scheduled Ancient Monument and a Grade I listed building and now operates as a major tourist attraction including spectacular landscaped grounds designed by Capability Brown. From the top of the ramparts and towers, the visitor can experience breath taking views of the English countryside. However, this does not really concern us as, like most of these impressive structures, Warwick Castle is haunted.

Warwick Castle is well known for its ghosts, with many guests and visitors to the castle seeing apparitions and shadows that they cannot explain. In 1628, Sir Fulke Greville was stabbed by one of his servants when the servant discovered that he would not benefit from Greville's will. After the deed, and horrified at his own actions, the servant cut his own throat and left Greville to die a very slow and painful death in the South Tower. It apparently took Greville a month to die, his anguish and pain compounded by the surgeon's insistence on packing the wound with mutton fat. Many visitors have reported hearing his moans for help. Witnesses have also reported catching fleeting glimpses of his sad shape haunting the Watergate Tower, or, the ghost tower, as it is ominously known.

In the dungeon, growls are often heard, and people have encountered a malevolent spirit, said to be an elementary who manifests into an aggressive human form, while elsewhere extreme fluctuations in temperature, light anomalies and physical sensations of being pushed and grabbed are all commonly reported.

One of the more famous ghosts of Warwick Castle is that of a large black dog with red eyes and foaming mouth. This devil-dog is believed to be the result of a curse placed on the castle by a servant by the name of Moll Bloxham. She was caught stealing from the Earl and was publically tortured and shamed for her deeds. Not long after, it is said that the dog appeared and started to cause havoc within the castle grounds.

In 2009 the *Birmingham Mail* reported that work on a new tourist attraction at the castle was halted after builders working on the new dungeon attraction claimed to be subject to ghostly encounters. The exhibition, which included a torture chamber, would have actors dressing up as ghosts and creatures from the dead to create a spooky atmosphere for visitors. However, site manager Paul Woodfield was left terrified when he spotted a strange figure in the hallways at the site. He was so scared he immediately dropped his tools and ran away in fear. "When we started clearing out the site for the new dungeon, which is in what used to be the castle's armory, I started to notice some pretty strange things. I kept smelling lavender which, for a building site, was very odd indeed. Later that day I saw a tall, slim man wearing some kind of tunic and trousers walking out toward the doorway."

At the time, two mediums who visited the castle reported seeing a woman hovering around one of the doorways in the new dungeon area. They later suggested that the woman could have been the ghost of Frances 'Daisy' Greville, the

Countess of Warwick and mistress to King Edward VII. They also noted a "general sense of fear and negative atmosphere".

As recently as 2016, Mariehanna Dickson took a photograph in the castle's Kenilworth room, a place reputed to be haunted by the ghost of a little girl. In the shot a small figure appears to be standing next to the window, but Dickson was completely alone at the time and later stated that she "was all alone in the room because it was early and there weren't many visitors around. When I got home I was reading the plaque on my camera and noticed a strange figure in the reflection of the shot. At first I thought it must have been one of the wax work figures in the castle, but when I called them they said there were no models in that room. I was so intrigued I called them to ask if anyone else could have been in the room without my knowledge, but they said they checked the CCTV and it showed me taking the picture in a completely empty room."

WHITTINGTON CASTLE
Shropshire
....
www.whittingtoncastle.co.uk

Whittington Castle in northern Shropshire was originally a motte-and-bailey castle, but this was replaced in the thirteenth century by a more substantial structure. Strikingly picturesque and romantic, it was a place of bitter border warfare, romance and legend. During the Civil War it was a Royalist stronghold until taken in 1643 by Cromwell's Roundheads and over the years it has seen many changes. As a result, it is a favorite for paranormal investigators and ghost hunters alike.

Ghostly sightings at the castle include a hooded figure under the castle gateway, a phantom blacksmith in a worn leather apron, and the faces of ghostly children, which are spookily seen peering out of an upstairs window. Legend has it they died when a cursed Elizabethan chest was opened and the curse released. There is also a guard room that some staff members refuse to enter.

Sue Ellis, manager of the castle, thinks there may be a more grounded explanation to this fear than ghosts. She says, "It is interesting what happens, but sometimes you wonder if it's because people are sitting in the dark. I think sometimes that creates a bit of apprehension and perhaps you start seeing things because your eyes aren't used to being in the pitch black. It does get very, very dark in the guard room, and so that's a bit scary in itself."

Having said this, even Ellis admits and there are things that simply cannot be explained including a vigil that once was held in the court room which, unknown to most, was once an ironing room. She explained that "We did a planchette, which is where you put a pencil in a block of wood and see if it draws anything. When it had finished, it did look like an old iron, but then the sceptic in me says maybe if the pencil was swinging it would just draw a triangle, and it could have just been a triangle.

In addition she noted:

We had a photo taken during one of our vigils that shows a spirit person in the corner of our bookshop. There's no room for a person to get into that corner, and I was in the room a minute after the picture was taken and there was no one there. Then we've had noises and a strange incident where there were a lot of children and we were playing with a ball in the old schoolroom and it was coming back to the same person each time, as though the floor was sloping. There was no real explanation.

SEVEN

NORTH WEST ENGLAND

ASKERTON CASTLE

Cumbria

....

http://askertoncastle.co.uk/history

Built around 1290 in the parish of Askerton in Cumbria, Askerton Castle was originally an unfortified manor. In the late fifteenth century, Thomas Lord Dacre built two crenellated towers on either end of the hall range, probably more so for increasing the living space than for any serious military or defensive purposes. A third tower may have been constructed on the north-west corner of the castle, but this is now long gone. It was renovated by architect Anthony Salvin in the 1850s and is now a Grade I listed building.

It is said to be haunted by the vengeful ghost of May Marye, who was murdered by a lover. Now she exacts revenge on the living by jumping on the backs of passing horses and terrifying their riders. It has been reported that she once engaged a rider in conversation, making him swear on his life that the topic of discussion would never be revealed to anyone.

CARLISLE CASTLE
Cumbria
....

www.english-heritage.org.uk/visit/places/carlisle-castle

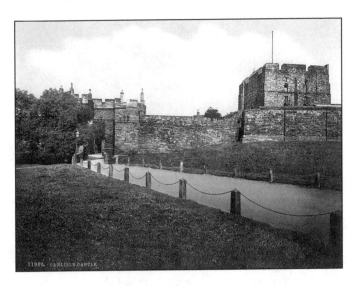

Over 900 years old and the scene of many significant historical episodes in British history, Carlisle Castle is situated in Cumbria close to the ruins of Hadrian's Wall. First built to keep the northern border of England secure from the threat of invasion from Scotland during the reign of William II of England, the son of William the Conqueror, it was constructed in 1093 when Cumberland (the original name for north and west Cumbria) was still considered a part of Scotland and it sits on the site of an old Roman fort.

Given the castle's history it is not surprising that the majority of ghost sightings are of a military nature. For instance, the apparitions of two medieval soldiers have been reported on the top floor of the keep while a ghostly sentry sits on guard just inside the archway of the inner keep.

The ghost of King Stephen is said to lean against the wall in the upper keep next to the model of the City of Carlisle and the spirit of an old caretaker has been seen sitting in a chair near the old bell. Interestingly, there is a picture of him in life sitting at Queen Mary's Table in the keep. As well, a black shadowy figure who wanders around in the inner keep has been reported by staff members and visitors alike.

A yeoman of an indeterminate era has been sighted walking up and down the pathway running in front of the cellblock toward the old Regimental Headquarters. One time it was reported that a caretaker doing his rounds met an apparently lost soldier on the stairs in Ypres block and when he told the soldier which way he needed to go he realized he was wearing the wrong uniform for the period.

Continuing with the military theme that seems to pervade this castle, it was reported that on one occasion, when locking Ypres block for the night, a Territorial Army Sergeant Major noticed that a light had been left on in the top-floor classroom. A corporal ran back upstairs and opened the classroom door to find it in darkness. Opening a window, he shouted down to the Sergeant Major that the light was off, only to be told that it wasn't. The corporal apparently made a hasty retreat.

In Cumbria's Military Museum, which is located within the castle grounds, several unexplained happenings have occurred including alarms being set off, even after an electrician replaced a faulty sensor, footsteps that can be heard upstairs when the place is empty, and on the back stairs a seemingly playful ghost pretends to push people down the stairs but then pulls them back as if playing a joke.

And, according to Richard Jones in his book *Haunted Castles of Britain and Ireland*: "In the 1830s during the construction of a parade ground and barracks, demolition work uncovered the skeleton of a lady bricked into one of the keep's second-story walls. Three rings upon the bony digits of her fingers and remnants of her silk, tartan dress were evident. There were no clues to her identity, although there was considerable speculation that she may have been walled up alive. The opening of her tomb, however, appears to have roused her revenant, for in 1842 a sentry on guard duty in the keep challenged the figure of a woman who approached him in the early hours of one morning. As she ignored him, he shouted to rouse his fellow guardsmen. Then, raising his bayonet, he charged at the figure. Just as he reached her, the woman simply melted into thin air, whereupon the soldier fainted clean away. Although his comrades did manage to revive him, such was the shock to his system that, having told them what had happened, he promptly fell back and died."

DACRE CASTLE

Cumbria

....

www.visitcumbria.com/pen/dacre-castle

A moated tower house that was constructed in the mid-fourteenth century, probably by Margaret Multon, Baroness Multon of Gilsland, as a form of defense against the threat of Scottish invasion and raids, it remained in the Dacre family until the seventeenth century. Renovated during the 1960s after periods of disrepair, the castle is now used as a private home although it does appear to have some other-worldly residents as well.

In the fifteenth century, Sir Guy Dacre fell in love with a girl called Eloise, the daughter of a French nobleman. She snubbed his advances, so he enlisted the help of his Italian tutor to help win her. Sadly though, the tutor had an affair with Eloise while Sir Guy was away fighting in Scotland.

When he returned she agreed to marry him, although he was still unaware of this affair. Sir Guy once again left to fight in Scotland and entrusted the castle to a loyal friend, Lyulph, who soon learned of the affair. The lovers left the castle and moved to York, and Lyulph told Sir Guy about what he learned.

Sir Guy set off after them and brought Eloise back to his castle where he locked her in a dungeon. In the dungeon, she found her Italian lover chained to the wall, as Lyulph had previously captured him. When she tried to kiss him, his head rolled from his shoulders. Lyulph had cut off his head and then set him in the dungeon. Eloise was cruelly kept captive in the cell beside the rotting corpse of her lover and eventually went mad and then died. Not surprisingly, her ghost is now said to haunt the castle.

It is also said that the site of Dacre Castle was the meeting place of three kings in ancient times who met to arrange a peace treaty with the Vikings. Their regretful ghosts make an appearance at the castle to this day.

LEASOWE CASTLE
Cheshire
....
http://leasowecastle.com

Believed to have been built for Ferdinando Stanley, 5th Earl of Derby, in 1593, the castle became abandoned by 1700 and became known as Mockbeggar Hall, a term often used for a decorative but derelict building. In 1821 it was purchased by the Cust family and after 1826 it was used for some years as a hotel. Between 1911 and 1970, it operated as a railway convalescent home, and between 1974 and 1980 it was owned by the Wirral Borough Council. Reopening as a hotel in 1982, it is now a popular wedding venue with around fifty bedrooms.

There are a number of accounts of paranormal and ghostly activity at the castle including, many years ago, a family feud ending with a man and his child being imprisoned in one of the rooms. Rather than having to face reprisals, the man killed his son and then committed suicide. To this day many guests staying in this room have reported seeing the two ghostly figures.

Guests have also reported strange feelings and unexplained noises have also been heard on the stairs. Another ghostly presence is one who appeared after a fire destroyed one of the buildings. This phantom is said to be seen at waist level on the floor because, when it was rebuilt, the floor was raised to a different level. There are also other rumors regarding a number of secret passages running throughout the building and it is said that these passages are also haunted.

LOWTHER CASTLE
Cumbria

....

www.lowthercastle.org

A castellated mansion built by Robert Smirke for William Lowther, 1st Earl of Lonsdale between 1806 and 1814, Lowther Hall, for all its appearances, is nothing but a shell these days, although its previous grandeur is obvious to all those who visit. Sadly the estate and castle fell into disrepair when Hugh Lowther, the 5th Earl of Lonsdale, wasted the family fortune on his overly lavish lifestyle. As a result he was forced to abandon the castle and move into more modest accommodation and it was closed in 1937. During the Second World War it was used by a tank regiment, and by 1957 its roof was removed leaving the shell we see today.

It is reputed to be haunted by Sir James Lowther, who, while stuck in an unhappy arranged marriage, fell in love with a local farmer's daughter. Sadly she died suddenly. Sir James kept the body, leaving it in bed and forbidding his servants to mention her. It is said that he would even dress her himself and seat her at the dining table with him. Finally she was placed in a coffin with a glass lid which he put in a cupboard so he could look at her, although after a while the body became so putrid it needed to be buried. The ghost of Sir James is said to reappear when the moon is full on the anniversary of his burial in the form of "Wicked Jemmy," seated high on a carriage and driving maniacally through the parkland while frantically whipping his horses. Of the girl, no one knows?

More recently visitors to the castle have reported seeing a figure in one of the upper windows of the castle. However, as previously mentioned, the castle is an empty shell with no upper floors and no way of reaching the windows where the figure has been seen. Who she is is a complete mystery. Is it possible that Sir James's tragic lost-love still watches for him over the years?

MUNCASTER CASTLE
Cumbria

....

www.muncaster.co.uk

Originally known as Mulcaster or Molecaster (1190) and Mulecaster (1236), Muncaster Castle, which overlooks the Esk River, is suspected to lie on foundations dating back to Roman times. The Muncaster estate itself was granted to Alan de Penitone in 1208 along with the oldest parts of the castle including the Great Hall and the fourteenth-century *pele* tower, a watch tower fortification unique to the English Scottish border region. It is owned by the Pennington families who have lived there for at least 800 years.

In 1464, Sir John Pennington gave Henry VI shelter after he was found wandering aimlessly after the defeat at the Battle of Hexham. On his departure, Henry left his drinking bowl as a sign of gratitude telling Pennington that as long as the bowl remained unbroken then the Pennington family would continue to live and thrive in the castle. The bowl remains intact to this very day and is known as the "Luck of Muncaster." And not only this, but as one would expect for such an ancient place, there are numerous reports of ghostly happenings within the castle walls.

The most haunted area is reputed to be the Tapestry Room. Visitors have reported the sound of a baby crying and a soft singing, which is believed to be a mother or a nanny soothing an upset child, as the room was previously used as a nursery. Other reports include disembodied footsteps, dragging sounds, rattling of the door handle in the middle of the night, the door opening, unexplained drops in temperature, frightening dark shadowy masses and the feeling of someone sitting down on the bed. As well, people often report an overwhelming feeling of someone else being in the room with them.

However, as haunted as this room appears to be, Muncaster Castle is more widely known for Tom Skelton, better known as Tom Fool. Tom was a jester at the castle until he died around 1600. Apparently he was a malicious and unpleasant character and would often direct people he didn't like toward quicksand when they asked for directions. He was also believed to have played a part in the beheading of a local carpenter who had an affair with Sir Ferdinand Pennington's daughter. The murder was thought to have been sanctioned by Pennington with Tom happy to assist so as to increase his status within castle social circles.

The current owners believe that Tom still resides within the great stone walls due to numerous strange happenings, especially those of a more sinister activity. Tom's portrait still hangs in the castle and, although he is never seen, one tourist to the castle had a frightening experience while looking at the portrait, stating that she could plainly hear footsteps on a stone floor walking up behind her. When she turned to see who it was she was stunned to realize that she was alone. She also claimed that the footsteps were clearly on a stone floor even though the stairs and corridor are fully carpeted these days.

But whereas Tom Fool remains hidden from view, the castle also boasts a White Lady. The White Lady, also known as the Muncaster Boggle, is regularly seen. She is thought to be the spirit of Mary Bragg who was a housekeeper during the early 1800s and who was murdered. Her body was later found in the Esk River but in such a bad state from the eels in the river that finding a cause of death was impossible. She is now often seen wandering the castle gardens and local roads, a forlorn spirit forever destined to be alone.

The castle's current owner, Patrick Gordon Duff Pennington, has ancestors who have been in residence since the early thirteenth century, noted in the 1995 television series *Castle Ghosts of England* that; "Sometimes when I open the doors, open the shutters in the mornings, people pull the doors out of my hands. The last curator used to see a Grey Lady walking up and down the passage outside our room."

Not only that, he also added, "The tapestry room, people have slept in there and asked to be moved. They hear people crying and they feel cold. They think it's a nasty place to be in and people who feel anything at all (are) not quite the same as when they went in."

Apparently in 1993 a group of ghost investigators set up a number of scientific instruments designed to capture evidence of ghosts. At 10:40 p.m. they felt the temperature drop dramatically. A minute later a vase began shaking and a loud thud was heard followed by three raps on a wall. The investigators also noticed a movement outside the door. They concluded that the castle was inhabited by supernatural energies.

NAWORTH CASTLE
Cumbria
....

www.naworth.co.uk

Also known as "Naward", Naworth Castle in Cumbria was the seat of the Barons Dacre and is thought to have been built in the late thirteenth century. It is a Grade I listed building with a square keep and bailey with its license to crenellate granted in 1335.

From 1939 to 1940 the castle was used by Rossall School in Lancashire due to the threat of German bombing. It is currently occupied by Philip Howard, brother of the thirteenth Earl of Carlisle.

The castle is said to be haunted by a White Lady, the spirit of a girl who was seduced by Lord Dacre without knowing his identity. She later became pregnant, and upon discovering Lord Dacres's rank and social standing, she realized they could never be together as she was of a lower class. As a result she was heartbroken and threw herself into a stream and drowned. The body was later discovered by Lord Dacre and his betrothed, and the dead girl's mother put a curse on Dacre, resulting in the death of him and his heirs. The ghost of the pregnant girl still haunts the castle, forever to remain alone and heartbroken.

PENDRAGON CASTLE
Cumbria
....
www.visitcumbria.com/evnp/pendragon-castle

Standing above a bend in the River Eden, Pendragon Castle was built in the twelfth century by Ranulph de Meschines and has the remains of a Norman keep with the later addition of a fourteenth-century turret as well as some further seventeenth-century additions. According to legend, the castle was built by Uther Pendragon, father of King Arthur, who is said to have unsuccessfully tried to divert the river to provide its moat. However, as entwined in the Arthurian legend as it seems, there is no evidence of any pre-Norman occupation of the site.

Interestingly Uther Pendragon is said to have been buried under a large mound near Uffington in Oxfordshire and his legend is closely tied to Tintagel in Cornwall. Of course, these are simply legends, but it does make one wonder how they came about in the first place.

In 1342 and again in 1541, the castle was attacked by Scottish raiding parties. After the latter attack, it was seriously damaged and remained a ruin until it was acquired by Lady Anne Clifford, who rebuilt it in 1660. Her successor, Thomas, the Earl of Thanet, had little use for it and removed anything of value so by the 1770s much of it was in ruins.

Interestingly, Hugh de Morville, one of the knights who murdered Thomas Beckett in 1170, is one of the castles more notable owners, and it is said that his ghost haunts the ruins. As well, some believe the ghost of Uther Pendragon also remains as legend suggests that it was here that he and a hundred of his men were poisoned by the Saxon invaders.

EIGHT

YORKSHIRE AND THE HUMBER

BOLTON CASTLE

Yorkshire

....

www.boltoncastle.co.uk

Built in the fourteenth century and located in Wensleydale in Yorkshire, Bolton Castle is a Grade I listed building and a Scheduled Ancient Monument, and remarkably has never been sold and is still in the ownership of the descendants of the Scrope family. Although damaged in the English Civil War, much of it remains and its gardens contain a maze, herb garden, wildflower meadow, rose garden and a vineyard.

After her defeat in Scotland at the Battle of Langside in 1568, Mary Queen of Scots stayed at Bolton for six months. She was allowed to roam the surrounding lands and often went hunting. Mary left Bolton Castle in January 1569, being taken to Tutbury in Staffordshire, where she spent much of her next eighteen years before execution in 1587.

It is said that Mary's ghost still wanders the grounds and corridors of the castle, and there have been reports of a "Lady in the Dark Cloak", who has been seen by the current Lord Bolton, a former caretaker, and twice by a villager. Sightings of this mysterious ghost woman have also been recorded at the castle in old books, often claiming it to be the ghost of Mary, Queen of Scots.

Bolton Castle General Manager, Katie Boggis noted in an article in the *Harrogate Informer* of 25 October 2013 that, "the tale of the lady in the dark cloak is well known to the staff here at the estate. One evening Lord Bolton was locking up at about 5:30 p.m. when he saw a lady across the courtyard. She was going into the East Curtain in what he thought was a dark coat. Thinking that it was a visitor still looking round, he waited outside for five minutes for the lady to finish her tour, but still there was no sign of her. He went into the East Curtain to see what she was doing and found no one there. There is only one entrance and exit to the East Curtain, which he had been standing by throughout. Exactly the same thing happened, but this time in the chapel, a couple of years later."

CONISBROUGH CASTLE
South Yorkshire
....

www.english-heritage.org.uk/visit/places/conisbrough-castle

Initially built in the eleventh century by William de Warenne, the Earl of Surrey, after the Norman Conquest, Conisbrough Castle is a medieval fortification in South Yorkshire. Later, in the late twelfth century, Hamelin Plantagenet, the illegitimate son of Henry II, acquired the property by marriage and it was subsequently rebuilt in stone and remained in the family until the fourteenth century, despite being seized several times by the Crown.

The castle fell into ruin with its outer wall badly affected by subsidence, and its derelict state prevented it from involvement in the English Civil War. It was later purchased by the Duke of Leeds in 1737 and by the end of the nineteenth century it had become a tourist attraction. Interestingly, Sir Walter Scott used the location for his 1819 novel *Ivanhoe*. English

Heritage took over the management and control of the castle in 2008 and it continues to operate as a tourist attraction.

The spirit of a gray monk has been seen stalking the ruined curtain walls and the ghost of a White Lady has been seen at the top of the keep, where it is believed she was pushed over the edge to her death. As well, disembodied footsteps have been heard in the keep and peculiar lights have been reported from the chapel area of the castle.

HELMSLEY CASTLE

Yorkshire

....

www.english-heritage.org.uk/visit/places/helmsley-castle

A desolate and windswept ruin situated in the market town of Helmsley in North Yorkshire, Helmsley Castle was originally constructed in wood around 1120 by Walter l'Espec and later converted to stone. In 1478 it was sold to Richard, Duke of Gloucester who later became Richard III. During the English Civil War, it was besieged by Sir Thomas Fairfax although the defender, Sir Jordan Crosland held it for three months before surrendering. Parliament ordered the castle to be slighted and much of the walls, gates and part of the east tower were destroyed. It is now owned by the Feversham family of Duncombe Park, although in the care of English Heritage.

The castle is reputed to be haunted by the ghost of a soldier who is believed to have originated from around the time of the English Civil War. As well, the ghost of a Green Lady, her green dress rustling in the breeze, has also been seen inside and outside of the castle during the dead of night. And in another bizarre tale, strange pixie-like creatures have been reported wandering the castle grounds, as well as the surrounding countryside.

In 2008, a team of paranormal investigators from the Northern Ghost Research Investigation Team UK was invited to investigate the castle by English Heritage after staff had reported strange occurrences, and although they produced no concrete evidence, they reported some interesting phenomena including flashing lights, thrown stones, disembodied footsteps and objects moving of their own accord.

KNARESBOROUGH CASTLE
Yorkshire
....

www.harrogate.gov.uk/info/20153
/knaresborough_castle_and_museum

Overlooking the River Nidd in North Yorkshire, Knareborough Castle was first built around 1100 and there is documented evidence dating from 1130 referring to works carried out at the castle by Henry I. Interestingly, Hugh de Moreville and his followers took refuge in the castle during the 1170s after assassinating Thomas Becket.

King John took control of the castle in 1205 as it was an important northern fortress. It was later rebuilt between 1307 and 1312 by Edward I and later completed by Edward II. John of Gaunt later acquired the castle in 1372.

The castle was taken by Parliamentarian troops in 1644 during the English Civil War and was destroyed after an order from Parliament to dismantle all Royalist castles. The ruins are open to the public and are often used as a performing space.

The castle is haunted by the ghost of a man standing above the ghost of another person lying prone on the ground, with his right arm raised as if to strike the figure lying on the ground. These ghosts appear as misty indistinct shapes and not much is known about their respective origins.

MIDDLEHAM CASTLE
Yorkshire

....

www.english-heritage.org.uk/visit/places/middleham-castle

Once the childhood home of Richard III, Middleham Castle was originally constructed by Robert Fitzrandolph, 3rd Lord of Middleham.

In 1258, Mary Fitzrandolph inherited the castle and in 1260 she married Robert Neville. The Nevilles rose to become one of the most powerful families in England and held the castle until the late fifteenth century. On the accession of Edward IV in 1461, his younger brother Richard was made Duke of Gloucester and, at the age of thirteen, he entered Warwick's household at Middleham, remaining there until toward the end of 1468.

Richard became Protector of the Realm upon Edward IV's death in 1483. Later that year he was crowned Richard III, usurping his twelve-year-old nephew, Edward V. However, he spent little time at Middleham in his two-year reign and after his death in 1485, the castle remained in royal hands until the reign of James I, when it was sold. It fell into disrepair during the seventeenth century and although garrisoned during the English Civil War, saw no action. The ruins are now in the care of English Heritage.

In recent years there have been reports of the sounds of muffled sixteenth-century music emanating from the empty castle, while the ghostly sounds of battle come from outside the castle and a knight on horseback charges at those who hear them, only to fade away before making contact. As well, people have reported seeing an inexplicable blue light at the top of the south wall as well as the sound of ghostly solders marching.

Interestingly, the castle is reputed to be the site of a buried hoard of treasure and to find it one must run around the castle three times and where they stop the treasure will be found. Unfortunately no one knows exactly where to start, so the treasure remains hidden.

PICKERING CASTLE
North Yorkshire

....

www.english-heritage.org.uk/visit/places/pickering-castle/

Originally built by the Normans in 1069 as a timber and earth motte-and-bailey, it was later developed into a stone motte-and-bailey castle. It is situated in the Vale of Pickering with a steep cliff on the west side which would have made for a superb defensive position. In 1926, the Ministry of Works, which is now English Heritage, took over running of the castle and it remains particularly well preserved as it was one of the few castles not to be severely affected by the fifteenth-century Wars of the Roses and the English Civil War of the seventeenth century.

While the castle was used to maintain control of Northern England, it never really played a serious role in any of the

British wars and was used more often than not by various Kings while on hunting trips. However, despite its relatively peaceful existence, it does offer sanctuary to one ghostly inhabitant, that being a robed monk, whose faceless form drifts across the grounds toward the ruined keep, his hands outstretched as though carrying some invisible item. It has also been suggested by those who have been close enough to notice that his face is bloodied. And apart from that, there have been bizarre stories of weird pixie-like creatures that have been spotted around the castle itself.

PONTEFRACT CASTLE

Yorkshire

....

www.pontefractcastle.co.uk

Pontefract Castle is situated to the east of the town of Pontefract and was constructed in approximately 1070 by Ilbert de Lacy on land granted to him by William the Conqueror. It is the site of a series of famous sieges during the English Civil War. King Richard II is thought to have died there.

During the twelfth century, King Henry I confiscated the castle, although his successor, King John returned the castle to de Lacy in 1199 after he ascended the throne. Roger died in 1213 and was succeeded by his eldest son, John. However, the King once again took possession of the castle. In 1311 the castle passed by marriage to the estates of the House of Lancaster.

Hundreds of soldiers were killed or imprisoned in the castle during the Wars of the Roses, and the place had such a feared reputation that it was even mentioned in the works of Shakespeare. Given this, there is little wonder that it is rumored to be haunted.

The ghosts that haunt this ruined but nevertheless spectacular site include a dark and menacing spectral figure holding an axe who wanders around the ruins of the castle, and a ghostly black monk who walks from the castle kitchen toward the Queen's Tower in the late afternoons. Visitors have reported seeing a ghostly woman in gray holding a lantern near the castle gates as well as two ghostly children who have been sighted playing near the dungeon of the castle. There are also reports of various apparitions of other monks who seem to wander aimlessly through the ancient ruins.

RICHMOND CASTLE

Yorkshire

....

www.english-heritage.org.uk/visit/places/richmond-castle

RICHMOND CASTLE. 8J.51.

Rising above the River Swale, Richmond Castle was originally called Riche Mount, "the strong hill" and was built by Alan Rufus between 1070 and 1086 after the 'Harrying of the North', an ethnic cleansing event by the ruling Normans that depopulated large areas of Yorkshire. Evidence suggests the early castle was originally built from stone, unlike most Norman castles that began as wooden motte-and-bailey castles and later evolved to stone fortifications. Notably, it lacks the earthworks common among castles of the period.

In 1158 it was seized by Henry II of England and it is suspected that he completed the construction of the keep. At roughly the same time, the castle was also strengthened by the addition of towers and a barbican. However, by the end of the fourteenth century it had largely fallen out of use as a fortress and no more major improvements were added. By 1538 a survey noted that it was partly in ruins.

In 1855 a barracks block was built in the great courtyard as the castle became the headquarters of the North Yorkshire Militia. In addition, from 1908 to 1910, the castle was the home of Robert Baden-Powell, the founder of the Boy Scouts, while he commanded the Northern Territorial Army. The barracks were demolished in 1931. Today the castle is a Scheduled Monument and a Grade I listed building and comes under the care of English Heritage.

Legend suggests that the castle is in fact the final resting place of King Arthur and the Knights of the Round Table, who lie sleeping and awaiting the day when they will come back to defend the realm in England's greatest time of need. It is said that they were once discovered by a potter named Potter Thompson, who recognized Arthur due to the horn and legendary sword Excalibur, which were both resting on a nearby table. So as to prove his story, he decided to take Excalibur, however, as he started to remove the sword from its scabbard, the sleeping knights began to wake and he became frightened, running from the cave. Once outside he regained his composure and turned back toward the entrance only to find that it had completely disappeared. The secret entrance has never been found since.

But whereas this is a simple folklore story, another legend tells that a drummer boy was lost while investigating an underground tunnel and that his ghostly drumming is some-times heard around the castle. As well, in the late 1990s, one of the castle guides leaving the tower room noticed a ghost walking between two closed doors. The tower room is also said to experience poltergeist activity which was apparently brought on after the chimney was unblocked in the middle of the twentieth century. In addition, the ghost of a nun is said to walk around at night, knocking on bedroom doors.

RIPLEY CASTLE
Yorkshire
....
www.ripleycastle.co.uk

A Grade I listed country house roughly five kilometers north of Harrogate, Ripley Castle was constructed in the fourteenth century and has been the seat of the Ingleby baronets for over

700 years and 28 generations. First acquired by Sir Thomas Ingleby as dowry for marrying Edeline Thwenge, it has a long and illustrious history including Thomas' oldest son, also called Thomas, who saved the King from being gored by a wild boar and was knighted in honor of his bravery with a boar's head symbol as his crest. In 1548 Sir William Ingleby, who was High Sheriff of Yorkshire in 1564–65, added a tower to the building.

In 1603 Sir William Ingleby hosted James VI of Scotland when the king was on his way to his coronation as James I of England, and in 1605 he was involved in the Gunpowder Plot, when he allowed the plotters to stay at the castle. He was later arrested and charged with treason but was acquitted. During the Civil War the Ingleby's sided with Charles I although the castle remained largely untouched by war.

A tragic and forlorn figure dressed in nineteenth century clothes has been seen at the castle. She is said to be the ghost of Lady Alicia Ingelby, who lost her only two children to meningitis in the 1870s. People have reported seeing her figure walking toward the children's bedrooms before passing unimpeded through a locked door. Indeed, the present Lady Emma Ingelby would often be feeding her baby when, if the baby gave a whimper, she would feel a nudge and a tug at the bedclothes. Her husband, Sir Thomas Ingelby, noted, "She would feel someone tugging the bedclothes, as if saying, wake up, your baby needs you. In the same area a couple of our guides have seen a lady in 1870s dress walking across the hallway. We believe it is Lady Alicia Ingelby. She is a very benevolent ghost."

Apart from that, inside the topmost tower, a poltergeist is reputed to move children's toys and becomes disturbed at the sound of babies crying. As well, the priest hole where Frances Ingelby hid before he was captured and executed is said to be haunted by his ghostly presence. And as befits such a place, there are the stories of civil war soldiers, lined up and shot by Cromwell's firing squad after the battle at Marston Moor. Their ghosts are said to haunt the castle walls.

SCARBOROUGH CASTLE
Yorkshire
....
www.english-heritage.org.uk/visit/places/scarborough-castle

Scarborough Castle is situated on a rocky headland overlooking the North Sea and Scarborough in North Yorkshire. The present stone castle dates from the 1150s and was strengthen over the centuries to guard the Yorkshire coastline and the north of England from Scottish or continental invasion. It was fortified and defended during various civil wars, sieges and conflicts, indeed, in 1557 Thomas Stafford seized the castle and held it for three days, believing he could incite a popular revolt against Queen Mary. However, the castle was easily captured, and Stafford and his accomplices were executed.

10365. - SCARBOROUGH, THE CASTLE.

The conclusion of civil and continental wars in the seventeenth century led to its decline in importance, and it has been a ruin since the end of the English Civil War although, from the 1650s the castle also served as a prison and its prisoners included George Fox, founder of the Society of Friends (the Quakers). It is now a tourist attraction and managed by English Heritage.

Piers Gaveston, the 1st Earl of Cornwall who was beheaded in 1312, spent his last free days in the castle. His ghost is said to have returned to the last place where he saw peace and freedom and now it wanders the ruins, a solitary figure dressed in medieval clothes. One legend suggests that his ghost sometimes tries to lure visitors to the cliff edge before attempting to push them off.

It is not known why this ghost is said to be that of Gaveston, but it has been documented that the entity, which has been witnessed on numerous occasions, has a threatening presence and that "visitors have felt unnerved, even in broad daylight, while walking the battlements, suddenly overcome with a dreadful sense that they are not alone. It is quite enough to persuade them to quicken their pace."

SHERIFF HUTTON CASTLE
North Yorkshire
....
www.castlesfortsbattles.co.uk/yorkshire
/sheriff_hutton_castle.html

Sheriff Hutton Castle is a quadrangular castle built by John, Lord Neville in the late fourteenth century. A license to crenellate was granted by Richard II in 1382 that formally made it a castle. It was later inherited by Richard Neville, also known as Warwick the Kingmaker, who at one point was the richest and perhaps most powerful man in England. However, when Warwick died in 1471, Edward IV appropriated the castle and gave it to Richard, Duke of Gloucester, who later became Richard III.

During the sixteenth century, Henry VIII's illegitimate son Henry Fitzroy lived in the castle under the care of Cardinal Wolsey, although soon after it began to fall into a state of disrepair, remaining the property of the crown until sold in 1940 to textile baron Wilfred Wagstaff.

Although relatively quiet in supernatural terms, the castle does claim one unearthly inhabitant—a ghostly girl. Current owner Dr. Richard Howarth in an article in *Farmers Weekly* noted, "we have a benign ghost, Nancy, probably a former lady-in-waiting. Several people have seen her including my father, who was a down-to-earth Yorkshire farmer."

This lack of ghosts raises an interesting question. Why is it that some castles with similar histories to Sheriff Hutton castle are allegedly haunted by numerous ghosts whereas Sherriff Hutton is not? If anything, when one walks the lonely ruins of this once magnificent structure, one would suspect that it has a long and varied history of various ghosts and hauntings, and yet, it doesn't.

SKIPTON CASTLE

North Yorkshire

....

www.skiptoncastle.co.uk

Constructed in 1090 by Robert de Romille, Skipton Castle is one of the most complete and best preserved medieval castles in England. Originally a motte-and-bailey castle, it was later rebuilt in stone to withstand attacks by the Scots with the cliffs behind the castle making it an easily defended position. In 1310, Edward II granted the castle to Robert Clifford, who was appointed Lord Clifford of Skipton. He commissioned many improvements but died in the Battle of Bannockburn in 1314 before many of these additions could be completed.

During the English Civil War, the castle was the last Royalist bastion in the North, only yielding to Parliament after a three-year siege in 1645 when a surrender was negotiated between Oliver Cromwell and the defending Royalists. Legend has it that during the siege, sheep fleeces were hung over the walls to deaden the impact from the rounds of cannon fire and these days sheep fleeces feature in the town's coat of arms.

Cromwell ordered the castle to be slighted but it was later fully restored by Lady Anne Clifford and it remained the Clifford's principal seat until 1676. Lady Anne Clifford was the last of her family to own the castle.

With such a history one would expect, like other similar castles, that Skipton Castle would have a long and mysterious history of ghosts and supernatural happenings; however, somewhat unexpectedly, it is relatively quiet. However, this is not to say that it is completely uninhabited by ghostly presences as the spirit of a lady with red hair, who some believe to be Mary Queen of Scots, has been seen gazing forlornly out of the windows, while Lady Anne Clifford's spectral carriage is supposed to drive madly up the High Street, through the closed gates where it stops outside the door, where she will collect the spirit of the castle's owner upon their death.

Mark Whitaker and his partner Amanda Ledgar visited the castle in 2014 and took what can only be described as a quite compelling photograph, that of what appears to be a ghostly girl in a white floor length period dress and a bonnet that appears to float where her head would be. Oddly enough the figure appears to have visible arms and a visible neck.

Whitaker only noticed the figure when he got back to his home in Colne, Lancashire and noted, "It actually sent a shiver down my spine as I didn't see it until I transferred it to my computer. I think it's a ghost of a little girl of some kind, especially with what she is wearing. She has a dress and bonnet that I think is like what they would wear two or three hundred years ago."

He also added, "It looks like she is walking away from the picture past a wall that is only about two or three feet high, so she must be an infant. There would have been high infant mortality rates in that period. It creeps me out, it really does still just looking at it. Amanda always finds it creepy too."

SPOFFORTH CASTLE
Yorkshire
....

www.english-heritage.org.uk/visit/places/spofforth-castle

Built by Henry de Percy in the early fourteenth century after being given a license to crenellate a manor house on the site,

Spofforth Castle is a ruined, fortified manor house in North Yorkshire.

In 1408, the castle and Percy estate were confiscated after the failed rebellion against King Henry IV, and later given to Sir Thomas Rokeby. They were later restored but were lost again in 1461 when the Percys supported the losing side in the War of the Roses. The castle was eventually returned to the family but was reduced to ruins during the English Civil War.

Now run by English Heritage as a Grade II listed building, it has a number of ghostly tales associated with it including the apparition of a half-human form that has been seen falling to its death from the tallest tower. This bluish-white form is said to be seen standing on the tiny parapet at the top of the eighteenth-century tower of the ruined castle before hovering for a few moments and then falling to the grass path below. In 1969 a group of schoolchildren and their teacher witnessed the phenomena, as did two picnickers in 1973.

NINE

NORTH EAST ENGLAND

BAMBURGH CASTLE
Northumberland
....
www.bamburghcastle.com

Sitting high on a massive rock overlooking the North Sea, Bamburgh Castle is a Grade I listed building built by the

Normans. During the eleventh century, it was the property of Robert Earl of Northumberland when he came to disagreement with King William II, who besieged the castle. The Earl was subsequently captured as he tried to escape with the castle becoming the property of the monarchy. Consequently the castle underwent numerous additions and upgrades with the keep completed by Henry II.

During the Wars of the Roses, the castle was occupied by the Lancastrians. However, they relinquished the castle in 1464 to Richard Neville, Earl of Warwick, who subjected it to a nine-month siege until they surrendered. Today, the castle remains intact and is one of the finest in England. The Armstrong family currently resides in it, along with other spooky denizens of the dark.

A Pink Lady is said to haunt the castle. She is said to be a Northumbrian princess who wanted to marry her true love, but her father disapproved of him and his standing in life. To ensure the romance did not grow any stronger the father sent the suitor overseas hoping that it would all blow over in time. After some time, he told her that her lover had married someone else and that she should forget all about him. To cheer up the distraught girl, the king asked the castle seamstress to make a dress in her favorite color, pink. However, when it was completed, she put on the garment, then climbed on to the highest battlements and threw herself to her death on the rocks below. It is now said that the forlorn princess returns to the castle every seven years in her pink dress, wandering around, then making her way down the rocky path to the beach, where she stands on the sands forever awaiting the return of her lost love.

As well, a ghostly woman with a green cloak is sometimes seen falling from the top of the castle, but vanishes before she hits the ground, and a knight in armor is often heard stomping about the castle, sometimes rattling chains.

BARNARD CASTLE
County Durham
....
www.english-heritage.org.uk/visit/places/barnard-castle

BARNARD CASTLE. S.J.60.

A ruined medieval castle situated in County Durham, Barnard Castle is a Scheduled Ancient Monument and was designated a Grade I building in 1950. Dating back to

Norman times, it was built by Bernard Balliol between 1112 and 1132.

Somewhere around 1300, Edward I granted the castle to the Earl of Warwick, while in the fifteenth century, the castle passed by marriage to the Neville family who improved the estate and created a substantial and impressive castle. In 1477 during the Wars of the Roses, Richard, Duke of Gloucester, and later to become Richard III, took possession of the castle.

The Castle remained a significant military stronghold over the next century until 1569, and the "Rising of the North" plotted at the nearby Raby Castle, saw it come under siege by supporters of Mary Queen of Scots. For eleven days the castle held firm but, running low on provisions, was forced to surrender.

In 1626 the Crown sold the castle to Sir Henry Vane who decided to make nearby Raby Castle his principal residence. As a result, Barnard Castle was abandoned and quickly fell into disrepair, its contents and building materials salvaged for improvements at Raby castle. Today it is a scenic ruin with spectacular views over the River Tees and nearby town. It is also reputed to be haunted by the ghost of Lady Ann Day.

Little is known about Lady Ann except that she lived in the sixteenth century and was murdered at the castle at a young age, her body thrown unceremoniously from the battlements into the chilly waters of the River Tees. And although her murderers name is now lost in the mists of time, horrified onlookers and visitors to the castle have often witnessed a young woman dressed in white falling from the castle. Some have claimed that her fall is punctuated by a heart rendering scream but as she hits the water the sound stops and there is no splash.

In addition, many visitors have experienced uneasy feelings of dread when in the Round Tower. Whether this is connected to the death of Lady Ann Day is unknown.

BELLISTER CASTLE
Northumberland
....

www.heartofhadrianswall.com
/forts-and-castles/82-bellister-castle

Located on the south bank of the River Tyne, across from the town of Haltwhistle, Bellister Castle stands on a partly man-made mount and was owned by Robert de Ros and his descendants from 1191 to 1295. In 1312 Gerrald Salveyn acquired the property, but it was confiscated from him in about 1354. John de Blenkinsopp, the owner of nearby Blenkinsopp Castle is thought to have built its tower after he acquired the building in about 1480. In the 1830s it was converted into a mock Gothic house by the famous architect John Dobson and is now a private residence although owned by the National Trust who purchased it in 1975.

It is reputedly haunted by the Gray Man of Bellister, the ghost of a wandering minstrel who was given food and lodgings for the night in return for some tales and songs. However, Lord Blenkinsopp suspected that the man was either a thief or a spy and when the minstrel slipped outside instead of retiring for the night, it confirmed his fears. The minstrel was pursued by the servants and the lord's hounds who caught him on the banks of the river and tore him to pieces. Not only did his ghost haunt Lord Blenkinsopp for the rest of his life, but it also said to haunt the building and grounds with locals insisting that they hear the baying of hounds at night as well as the screams of an old man

Interestingly, there is an old Sycamore tree in front of the west side of the castle which is known as the hanging tree. It is believed that the tree was used for executing Royalist Cavaliers during the Civil War.

BOWES CASTLE
County Durham
....
www.english-heritage.org.uk/visit/places/bowes-castle

Located in County Durham, Bowes Castle was built in 1136 by Alan the Red, Count of Brittany, who also owned the nearby Richmond Castle. It stands on a late first century Roman fort that was designed to protect the road across the Pennine Mountains. In 1173 it was allegedly besieged by King William of Scotland and between 1314 and 1322, it was virtually destroyed. By 1325 it was reportedly in a state of ruins.

According to legend, near the end of the Roman occupation in England, the Roman garrison raided the local villages stealing everything of worth, including gold. Angered, the locals banded together and attacked the fort killing all the soldiers. However, when they went to retrieve their valuables they found the gold missing as the Romans had buried it somewhere. The gold has never been recovered and on the anniversary of the massacre, the ghosts of the garrison are said to appear at the castle to bury their stolen gold and treasure.

Paul Gater in his book *Ghosts at War* notes, "Legend has it that about three hundred years ago, a couple of local men spent the supposed anniversary night of the massacre among the ruins. Afterwards, they both claimed having seen a group of phantom Roman soldiers carrying a large chest of gold and burying it. Unfortunately they were unable to say where and both died violent deaths soon afterwards."

In recent times there have been reports from walkers in the area of seeing the ghostly soldiers in full uniform with helmets and shields as well as a standard that flies proudly in the wind. As well, there are regular sightings and reports of large, dark shadows that move around the castle, and with so much bloodshed at the place over the past, it comes as little surprise that it is considered haunted.

BLENKINSOPP CASTLE
Northumberland

....

www.blenkinsoppcastleinn.co.uk

Located in Greenhead, Northumberland, about a mile from Hadrian's Wall, Blenkinsopp Castle is a partly-ruined country mansion that incorporates the remains of a fourteenthcentury tower house. It is now a Grade I building and Scheduled Ancient Monument. It was previously owned by the Blenkinsopp family from the thirteenth century. However, by 1541 it was reported that the roof was in decay and the tower in poor repair, so the family abandoned it and moved to nearby Bellister Castle. It was later renovated in 1877 by William Blenkinsopp Coulson. In 1954 it was severely damaged by fire. It has only just recently come on the market again.

It is said that the castle is haunted by a phantom hound and a White Lady. The former is said to appear when the owner of the property is near death, while the White Lady is believed to be the ghost of the wife of Bryan de Blenkinsopp. Legend has it that she became upset upon hearing gossip that she had married him only for his money, so she hid the treasure which, caused her husband to lose his temper and, in a rage, he left the castle never to return. She waited for years for him to return but he never did and now she haunts the castle, guarding the treasure that she hid and still waiting in vain for his return.

It appears that the White Lady is now seen quite infrequently, however, a story associated with her concerns a family who were renting the premises. One night, after going to bed, the husband and wife were startled to hear screams coming from an adjoining room in which one of their children, a boy aged about eight, was sleeping. On entering the room, the couple found the boy sitting on the bed trembling and white faced. When they asked him what had happened, he could only stammer the words "The White Lady! The White Lady!"

Confused, the parents asked him about this White Lady, pointing out that the room was empty.

The parents concluded that the boy had probably had a nightmare and in time managed to get him back to sleep. However, for three successive nights they were disturbed in the same manner, the boy repeating the same story with little variation. In the end they had no option but to move the terrified child to another room, although the boy, it is said, would never enter any part of the old castle on his own after his frightening experience.

CASTLE KEEP

Newcastle

....

www.newcastlecastle.co.uk

Castle Keep is one of the finest surviving examples of a Norman keep in England and is a part of the castle, Newcastle, a medieval fortification in Newcastle-upon-Tyne. It, and the Black Gate, a fortified gatehouse, are the most prominent remaining structures on the site which is located on a steep-sided promontory which overlooks the River Tyne.

Castle Keep was built by Henry II between 1172 and 1177 with the Black Gate added by Henry III between 1247 and 1250. In 1589, during the reign of Queen Elizabeth, the castle was described as being in ruins although during the English Civil War, the Royalist mayor of Newcastle, Sir John Marley, repaired the keep and probably also refortified the castle. In 1644 the Scottish Army crossed the border in support of the Parliamentarians and besieged Newcastle for three months until the garrison surrendered. During the sixteenth to the eighteenth century, the keep was used as a prison and by 1800 there were a large number of houses within the boundaries of the castle.

Today the Castle Keep is a visitor attraction and is a Grade I building, open to the public almost every day of the year.

Numerous people have reported inexplicable ghostly happenings in Castle Keep, including the sounds of ghostly footsteps in the narrow corridors, to unexplained mists which visitors have captured on camera. Visitors also have complained of experiencing cold spots that appear and disappear without any reason as well as being touched by invisible hands.

The Queens Chamber is reputed to be the most haunted area, with many people reporting that they have heard chanting in the chamber, similar to the chants of monks. A ghostly woman has been seen many times in the chamber as well as in the chapel, and visitors have reported being attacked, scratched, and shoved.

The Keep's most famous ghost, however, is known as the "Poppy Girl." Legend suggests she is the ghost of a flower girl who was sent to prison because she owed some people money. While she was in prison she was raped and beaten to death by the male prisoners. She is often seen on the stairs of the keep and it is said that when she is nearby, a scent of flowers is in the air.

CHILLINGHAM CASTLE
Northumberland
....
www.chillingham-castle.com

Originally a monastery in the late twelfth century, Chillingham Castle is a medieval castle in the northern part of Northumberland. At first glimpse the staid old building could have been taken straight from a fairy tale, however the reality is somewhat more gruesome.

In 1344 a License to crenellate was issued by King Edward III to allow battlements to be built, effectively upgrading the stronghold to a fully fortified castle as it was the first line of defense against invading Scots. Renovations included a dungeon where prisoners from this conflict were sealed up, interrogated, and subjected to horrific tortures. Captured soldiers would have their arms and legs broken before being tossed down through a trap door, falling twenty feet into the dungeon below to die a slow and painful death.

In 1617, as relations between England and Scotland became peaceful, James I stayed at the castle and, as the need for a military presence in the north diminished, the castle was gradually transformed with the moat filled and battlements converted into residential wings.

During the second world war, the castle was used as an army barracks with the decorative wood interior stripped out and burned by the soldiers billeted there. After the war, the castle fell into disrepair with lead removed from the roof, resulting in extensive water damage to large parts of the building. These days the castle has been renovated and certain sections are open to the public.

Chillingham Castle's dungeons are a thing of legend with horrific stories of Scottish prisoners trapped in the dungeon who were so starved that they resorted to eating the dead. And just as horrific, the most desperate were said to have resorted to eating their own flesh. As such, it doesn't take a great stretch of imagination to suggest that the place is haunted, and the castle does not disappoint in this respect as the amount of supernatural experiences people have reported during their visits to the castle are astounding.

One of the castle's most famous ghosts is the Blue Boy. He is believed to be the spirit of a young child who was found bricked up along with some documents and a few scraps of blue clothing. The bones of his fingers had been worn away to the nubs, suggesting that he had been bricked in while alive and that he had tried to scratch his way out. People have reported hearing the terrifying screams of the boy in the Pink Bedroom before the sound stops and the spirit of the boy, dressed in blue and surrounded by a bright aura would approach the old four-poster bed. After the discovery of his body in the 1920s, his bones were interred in the local graveyard and sightings of his ghost ceased. However, visitors who sleep in the Pink Bedroom often report that one wall of the room lights up with bright flashes of blue light suggesting that his spirit is still active.

Lady Mary Berkeley is another of the castle's ghosts. She is seldom seen but the rustle of her dress is often heard by visitors as she crosses the living room, apparently searching for her errant husband who seduced and ran off with his wife's younger sister in the 1600s, leaving Mary and her baby girl alone in the castle.

In the inner pantry a frail figure in white sometimes appears to visitors. She is known as the White Pantry Ghost and is suspected of having died from poisoning. The family silver used to be stored in the room where she is seen, and a footman was employed to sleep here and guard it. One night, when the footman had turned in to sleep, he was approached by a very pale-looking lady in white who asked him for some water. Thinking it was one of the castle guests he turned to get her some when he remembered he was locked in and no visitor could have possibly entered. When he turned back, the apparition had disappeared. It is thought her longing for water suggests that she was poisoned.

Beside the great hall, the voices of two men are often heard talking although no one can make out what they are talking about. They stop talking if one makes an effort to trace them, suggesting that whoever the ghosts are, they are aware of what is going on around them. Visitors to the castle have also reported having their hair pulled, arms scratched and even being bitten by unseen assailants while in the dark of its stone walls and corridors.

DUNSTANBURGH CASTLE
Northumberland
....
*www.english-heritage.org.uk/visit/places
/dunstanburgh-castle*

Standing on a rocky outcrop overlooking the sea on its eastern flank, Dunstanburgh Castle is a serene and pictur-esque ruin dating back to the fourteenth century. Built by Earl Thomas of Lancaster between 1313 and 1322 and tak-ing advantage of the site's natural defenses and the existing earthworks of an Iron Age fort, it served as a secure refuge for those opposed to King Edward II, as well as serving as a statement of the Earl's influence. Thomas however, was captured by Royalists and executed on a hill north of St John's Priory. It is rumored that the executioner was inexperienced and that it took him eleven blows to sever Thomas's head with the axe. The castle then became the property of the Crown. The Earl's ghost is now said to haunt the ruins of the castle carrying his mutilated head.

In the 1380s, John of Gaunt, the Duke of Lancaster, bolstered the castle's already formidable defenses due to the threat of Scottish attacks and from the peasant uprisings of 1381. The castle continued to be maintained during the fifteenth century by the Crown and was part of the strategic northern stronghold during the Wars of the Roses, although it changed hands between the rival Lancastrian and Yorkist factions on several occasions. Although the castle survived, it never quite recovered from the sieges and by the sixteenth century it had fallen into disrepair. It was finally sold off to private owners in 1604 with the threat from the Scottish border abating.

The Earl's ghost has been seen around the castle carrying his mangled head under his arm, his face bearing the pain and horror he suffered when the executioner delivered the final blow that took his life. As well, the ghost of Margaret of Anjou, wife of King Henry VI, has also been reported drifting across the castle grounds. Another alleged resident of the castle is the ghost of Sir Guy the Seeker.

According to the Arthurian legend, Sir Guy the Seeker was a chivalrous knight who, while riding along the Northumberland coast one day, found himself caught in a raging storm and sought shelter within the ruins of Dunstanburgh Castle. Finding sanctuary within its massive gatehouse, Sir Guy was suddenly confronted by a gruesome creature dressed in white who invited him to follow it to be rewarded by a beauty bright.

Intrigued, Sir Guy followed the figure up a winding staircase and into a room that contained hundreds of sleeping knights with their horses. In the center of the room was a sparkling casket in which a beautiful maiden lay sleeping. However, on each side of the maiden were serpents, one holding a sword, the other a horn. Sir Guy was told that he could wake the lady from her slumber, but he must choose either the sword or the horn as only one of them could awaken her. Fatefully, Sir Guy chose the horn and blew it. Suddenly, the sleeping knights came to life and attacked him. As they did, the room began to swirl and he felt himself slipping into unconsciousness. As he did, the figure in white appeared taunting him with a voice that echoed inside his head "Now shame on the coward who sounded a horn, and the knight who sheathed a sword."

When Sir Guy regained consciousness, he was lying near the ruins of the gatehouse and from that day on he was determined to find the sleeping maiden again and he spent the rest of his life searching the castle for the room in which she had lain. It became an obsession as he searched every corner of the desolate ruin. And yet, for all his determination he never again found the room in which she lay, and he died a broken, lonely old man. It is said that his ghost haunts the castle, fated to search the lonely ruins forever.

DURHAM CASTLE
County Durham

....

www.durhamworldheritagesite.com/architecture/castle

Built in the eleventh century as a northern-Norman military stronghold following the Norman Invasion of 1066, Durham Castle is an example of the early motte-and-bailey castle. The castle stands on top of a hill above the River Wear, opposite Durham Cathedral, and possesses a large Great Hall, created by Bishop Antony Bek in the early fourteenth century. Over the centuries it has been the residence of the Bishops of Durham who added to the buildings and altered them to suit the needs over time. It has been occupied since 1840 by University College, Durham and generally open to the public through guided tours as it is a working building and the home to over 100 students.

The most famous of ghosts in the castle is said to exist on a great wooden staircase known as the Black Staircase. This impressive structure lies between the Great Hall and Bishop Pudsey's building and is constructed of a dark stained wood, hence the nickname. It was built around 1662 and stands sixty feet in height. The ghost that haunts this area is known to all as the Grey Lady of Durham Castle and it is suspected that she was the wife of one of the former bishops who once resided there. It is said that one day, for some unknown reason, feeling suicidal, she climbed the staircase and threw herself off. Visitors and staff alike have reported seeing her tragic figure although her presence is felt more often than not. Interestingly, the Grey Lady is said to float above the steps as their level has changed over the years.

In addition, another ghostly presence is said to haunt the Owengate area of the complex. This is rumored to be the spirit of a university professor who also threw himself down a flight of stairs, this time a set of stone stairs elsewhere in the castle. Maybe, as a visitor, one should be careful on the stairs within the castle.

FEATHERSTONE CASTLE
Northumberland
....

www.heartofhadrianswall.com
/forts-and-castles/83-featherstone-castle

A Grade I manor house, which belonged to the Featherstonehaugh family, Featherstone Castle played a central role in the battles between the English and the Scots. Originally a thirteenth-century hall house, a square three-story pele tower was added in 1330 by Thomas de Featherstonehaugh to allow it castle status.

Following the start of World War I, the castle was leased to a preparatory school. During World War II it was used by a school from Rugby, although from 1942 a prisoner of war camp was also established. It is now used as a self-catering residential center for young people and students, and although it is somewhat lacking in supernatural stories, its Jacobean frontage certainly looks the part.

Having said that, the ghost story associated with Featherstone castle is interesting all the same as, in the seventeenth century, Baron Featherstonehaugh arranged for his daughter to marry, even though the daughter was in love with someone else. And, according to legend, when the wedding party left for the traditional hunt after the ceremony, they left the Baron behind to oversee arrangements for the banquet. However, when the party failed to return by midnight, the Baron began to fear the worst and while sitting alone at a table, he heard horses crossing the drawbridge. Overjoyed to hear them he leapt to his feet just as the doors opened and the party entered. However, to his consternation they made no sound and passed straight through the furniture and walls.

Later he was to learn that the wedding party had been ambushed and killed by the daughter's spurned lover and his family. Now on the 17th of January, the anniversary of the wedding, the ghostly wedding party can be seen riding toward the castle.

Apart from this, it is also said that a female ghost in a green and brown dress haunts the castle, gliding silently along the corridors, while the tormented spirit of Sir Reginald FitzUrse haunts a tower where he was held prisoner and starved to death

HAUGHTON CASTLE
Northumberland
....
www.haughtoncastle.com

A fortified mansion situated to the north of the village of Humshaugh, Haughton Castle was originally built in the thirteenth century as a tower house, although it was later enlarged and fortified in the fourteenth century when owned by Gerald

Widdrington. Sadly, by the sixteenth century the castle had fallen into disrepair and a survey of 1541 reported the roof and floors to be "decayed and gone."

In about 1640, the castle was acquired by the Smith family, although a further survey in 1715 again stated the building to be ruinous. However, significant alterations were carried out between 1816 and 1845 and the building was converted to a substantial mansion. Part of the castle served as a hospital during the Second World War and it is regarded as one of the best-preserved hall houses in the north of England

The castle is said to be haunted by the ghost of the head of the Armstrong clan, Archie Armstrong, who was captured in the sixteenth century and accidentally left to starve to death in the castle's dungeons. Apparently Sir Thomas Swinburne, the castle owner, had been summoned to York by the Chancellor, Lord Cardinal Wolsey and forgot that he had thrown Armstrong in the dungeon. By the time he remembered, Armstrong had gone three days without water or food, so he sped back and eventually reached the castle at midnight, exhausted. However, he was too late and when he opened the entrance to the dungeon, Armstrong was dead. His features were contorted with a look of horror and the flesh of his forearm had been gnawed away.

The ghost of Armstrong haunted the castle ever since with dreadful shrieks coming from the dungeon. As such a priest was brought in to exorcise the ghost, which he did with the help of a large black bible which he left in the building. However, years later after the ghost had been long forgotten, the bible was taken away for repair and immediately the shrieking resumed. The bible was hastily returned, and the fearful shrieking ceased.

It is said by some that Armstrong's ghost still haunts the castle, his shredded arm limp by his side as he stalks the lonely depths of the dungeon.

LINDISFARNE CASTLE
Northumberland

·················

www.nationaltrust.org.uk/lindisfarne-castle

Situated on a rocky mound, Lindisfarne Castle was built in the sixteenth century and is located on Holy Island, near Berwick-upon-Tweed. In 1542 Henry VIII ordered that the site be fortified against possible Scottish invasion and, as a result, a fort was built on Beblowe Crag, and this formed the basis of the present castle. Elizabeth I then carried out more work on the fort, strengthening its walls and providing gun platforms in 1570 and 1571. However, when James I came to power, he combined the Scottish and English thrones and the military status of the castle waned.

In the eighteenth century the castle was taken for a brief period by Jacobite rebels but was quickly recaptured by soldiers from Berwick. However, they managed to dig their way out of their prison and they hid for nine days close to nearby Bamburgh Castle before presumably escaping across the border. The castle is now a popular tourist attraction and can only be accessed from the mainland at low tide by means of a causeway.

In 635, St Aiden founded Lindisfarne Priory on Holy Island and in 664, St Cuthbert visited the island for the first time. In 685 he was consecrated as Bishop of Lindisfarne and when he later died, he was buried on the island. Some years later his casket was reopened and his corpse was apparently found not to have decomposed. As a result hundreds of people began to come to Lindisfarne as a pilgrimage. However, fearing Viking raiders, the body was relocated, as were other important relics.

These days there are reports of St Cuthbert's ghost wandering the island dressed in simple robes. He has been seen in the grounds of the priory and the castle, as well as sitting by the shore making what is known as 'Cuddy's Beads', fossilized sea lilies which were strung together and used as necklaces or, in some cases, rosaries.

St Cuthbert, however, is not the only ghost that has been seen on the island. There have also been reports of a Cromwellian soldier in the castle and apparitions of monks in the priory grounds. As well, it has been reported that a large white hound sometimes leaps from the castle and runs toward people before slinking back to the castle and disappearing.

PRUDHOE CASTLE
Northumberland

....

www.english-heritage.org.uk/visit/places/prudhoe-castle

Built on the site of a previous Norman motte-and-bailey, Prudhoe Castle is situated on the south bank of the River Tyne at Prudhoe, Northumberland. It was built sometime in the mid-eleventh century by Robert d'Umfraville who replaced the wooden palisade with a massive rampart of clay and stones and subsequently constructed a stone curtain wall and gatehouse. Later, in 1173 William the Lion of Scotland invaded the North East but the d'Umfraville family refused to support him. As a result the Scottish Army tried unsuccessfully to take Prudhoe Castle. The following year the castle was once again attacked but the garrison had been strengthened and once again the Scots were repelled.

Over the subsequent years it was occupied by the d'Umfraville family until 1398 when the castle passed to the Percy family who, apart from a period of time when it was forfeited to the Crown, lived there until 1536 although by 1537 it was reported as being in poor shape. The castle was again restored by Thomas Percy, the 7th Earl in about 1557. However, he was convicted of taking part in the Rising of the North in 1569, and although he escaped, he was recaptured and executed in 1572. After this, numerous persons tenanted the castle, but by 1776 it was reported as being ruinous.

Between 1808 and 1817, substantial repairs were made to the castle and in 1966 the castle was given to the Crown. It is now under the control of English Heritage and is open to the public.

The castle is reputed to be haunted by the ghost of a knight with a large beard as well the spirit of a Grey Lady. Who she is remains a matter of speculation although there is a road in a nearby estate named Grey Lady Walk as a reference to the ghost.

Interestingly, Prudhoe is said to have a secret underground passage linking it with Bywell Castle about three miles away. However, this means that at some point it would have to go under the River Tyne and as the tunnel has never been uncovered it is doubtful that it ever existed.

In November 2016, David Wilkins, took a number of photographs at the castle, and one showed a wispy white apparition that appeared to take the shape of a girl turning to face the camera. Photographs taken before and after show nothing more than the castle itself. David's wife Brenda said of the photograph; "I had goosebumps the moment he mentioned it and as soon as I saw the picture I saw the little girl."

RABY CASTLE

County Durham

....

www.rabycastle.com

Constructed by John Neville, 3rd Baron Neville de Raby, between 1367 and 1390 near Staindrop in County Durham, Raby Castle was the birth place of Cecily Neville, the mother of Kings Edward IV and Richard III. An imposing fortress composed of a curtain wall with eight massive towers that surround the central keep, its original defensive purpose is evident in that the only entrance is through a fortified gateway accessed by a narrow path across a moat, although these days the moat has been converted to a lake and the curtain wall reduced to a simple parapet.

The Nevilles held the castle until 1569 when it was forfeited to the Crown following Neville support for the failed Rising of the North. The castle remained in Crown hands until 1626 when it was purchased by Sir Henry Vane the Elder, Treasurer to Charles I. Extensive alterations were carried out in the seventeenth and eighteenth centuries and, although a private home and the seat of the Vane family, it is a Grade I building and open to the public on a seasonal basis.

The ghost of Charles Neville, the Sixth Earl of Westmorland, has been seen on the staircase and in the Baron's Hall where, in 1569, he met with the Percy family of Northumberland to plot the Rising of the North. Interestingly, although his ghost is said to haunt the castle, he is buried in Holland. It is said that his specter is angry at having lost his title, lands, and castle.

As well, an unidentified ghost has been seen entering the castle, vanishing as it reaches the gate, while a figure suspected to be Lady Barnard has been seen in the castle corridors at night, apparently knitting with white-hot needles, seething over the memory of her son Gilbert, who dared to marry against her wishes. She is said to be quite old looking with wild staring eyes that glow in the dark of night. When alive she was contemptuously known as Old Hell Cat, and in death it appears that she has not changed.

Another ghostly figure, this time a rather portly man, has been seen sitting at a desk in the library writing. However, his ghostly body ends at his shoulders and his head has been reported as lying on the table, it's ghastly lips moving as if dictating a letter or relaying instructions. This gruesome apparition is said to be that of Sir Henry Vane the Younger who died at the age of forty-nine, executed after a trumped up treason charge. It is said that he protested loudly while awaiting execution, so loudly that the sheriff in charge of the grisly spectacle ordered that trumpets be blown to drown out his words. Is it possible that in death he continues to protest his innocence?

WALWORTH CASTLE

County Durham

....

www.celticcastles.com/castles/walworth-castle

Situated at Walworth in County Durham, Walworth Castle is a Grade 1 building that was completed around 1600 for Thomas Jenison, Auditor General of Ireland, probably by Thomas Holt, a seventeenth-century architect who designed a number of buildings at the University of Oxford. The east and west wings were rebuilt during the reign of Elizabeth I and in 1759 the north wing was rebuilt. It is believed that King James VI of Scotland stayed at the castle at one stage. During the Second World War it was used as a prisoner of war camp and later was used as a girl's boarding school before being bought by the county council in 1950. It then opened as a hotel and has remained as such until the present.

The castle is reputed to be haunted by the ghost of a maid who fell pregnant to a lord of the manor at some time in the past. Instead of acknowledging the affair, the lord had the girl

bricked up in a wall, where a spiral staircase was being renovated and it is believed that it is her ghost that is often seen
walking along the corridor by the honeymoon suite as well as
suddenly appearing from the wall by the staircase.

The ghost of another young woman has also been seen
sitting in an armchair, however, it is unknown whether or
not she is the same girl. There have also been reports of footsteps on the stairs leading to one of the turrets, guests experiencing someone sitting on the edge of their beds when no
one is there, and chambermaids having their hair pulled.

WARKWORTH CASTLE
Northumberland
....

*www.english-heritage.org.uk/visit/places
/warkworth-castle-and-hermitage*

A stunning and commanding ruined medieval building on
a loop of the River Coquet, less than a mile from England's

north-east coast, it is thought to have been constructed by Prince Henry of Scotland in the mid-twelfth century. Located near the border of Scotland, the castle was often the subject of conflict and it switched ownership numerous times between the English and Scots.

In the late nineteenth century, it was refurbished and Anthony Salvin was commissioned to restore the keep. Alan Percy, 8th Duke of Northumberland, gave custody of the castle to the Office of Works in 1922 and since 1984 English Heritage has cared for the site, which is a Grade I building and a Scheduled Ancient Monument. Interestingly, JMW Turner painted a picture of the castle in 1799.

And with such a history, it is not surprising that the castle is considered haunted, even if only mildly so in comparison to other great stone structures that dot the landscape.

The ghost of Margaret Neville, known as the Grey Lady, has been seen drifting around one of the towers at Warkworth and the ghost of a young man has also been seen running along the castle walls. Who he is, no one knows. However, despite occasional visual ghostly activity, visitors to the castle seem more likely to encounter a disconcerting atmosphere and as Richard Jones notes in his book *Haunted Castles of Britain and Ireland*, "Its lower floors possess a distinctly chilling aura, and dogs show a marked reluctance to enter them; if they do, they become decidedly alarmed. Children entering its dark interior have also been known to fall under its strange spell, becoming silent and contemplative."

CONCLUSION

From the soaring grandeur of Arundel Castle to the brooding ruins of Ludlow Castle, England's long and illustrious history has been immersed in death, ambition, greed, treachery, and betrayal. Its castle walls have witnessed centuries of tragedy and bloodshed and the tormented and anguished wails of the forlorn dead still echo through the dark corridors, cells and rooms. It is, indeed, ripe with ghosts and stories of the supernatural.

But what is it that we are dealing with here? Let us have a look at a classic-style haunting. For instance, many people in England have reported seeing Roman soldiers marching by, although only from the waist up which suggests that these ghosts are marching along, not on an existing path, but one that existed many years in the past. This makes perfect sense and a great example of this sort of ghost is seen in the well-known tale of Harry Martindale, an apprentice plumber who, in 1953, was installing a heating system in the cellars of the Treasurer's House in York when he witnessed the ghosts of Roman centurions. He heard a horn in the distance and then a dishevelled Roman soldier on a horse emerged from the brick wall. This soldier was followed by others, all looking dejected and tired, carrying swords and spears. They appeared from the knees up, which suggests that they were walking on a road that was buried below them. It was later confirmed that an old Roman road was located fifteen inches below the cellar.

After this bizarre procession had passed, Martindale made a hasty escape from the cellar and sat at the top of the stairs quite bewildered, when an old curator saw him and asked if he'd seen the Roman soldiers.

Although Martindale's experience is rare—most people will spend their entire lives without seeing a ghost—a large percentage of the population believe that ghosts, in various forms, exist.

Throughout this book we have accepted that normal people genuinely see things that they believe are of a supernatural origin. However, as we have also seen, these ghostly occurrences do not always follow the same pattern, in fact, so different are these patterns that it is logical to assume that there are one or more types of ghosts, or one or more types of hauntings. And so it seems for our castle-ghosts of England. Whereas some are full apparitions, other are reported as nothing more than feelings, or wispy spots of mist, or even disembodied voices.

But where does this leave us? Are we any closer to understanding the phenomena that is a ghost? Does this apparent abundance of ghosts occur due to the rich and ancient history of the place? Why is it that some places that have suffered war, death, and disease are haunted whereas other places that have equally seen the same are not haunted? Why do some people see ghosts whereas others do not? And more to the point, how is it that so many people with no connection to each other and over such a length of time report similar ghostly happenings at the same places?

Surely all these witnesses cannot be lying and have simply invented their stories, even though these stories are almost exactly the same and occur over a period of years, if not decades. Does this legitimize their experiences and prove that ghosts do exist?

Or is it a case of us looking in the wrong direction? Is it possible that some people are predisposed to seeing ghosts? Are the imaginary friends of our childhood really imaginary, or are they in facts ghosts, entities that we as adults have somehow lost the ability to see?

And what of places that seem to convey a certain feeling, a certain depressing or ominous feeling? Without doubt everyone reading this book would have visited such a place, whether it be a morgue, a cemetery, an ancient battlefield or a dark, ruined castle. Who among us cannot say that they have walked into a room or wandered along a lonely road at night and felt the hairs on the back of their necks rise and their heart beat faster? Is this an evolutionary response to a once real threat but now lost in the mists of time, a lost human-sense, one that seems to have been abandoned in this new and maddeningly fast modern world?

Ghosts and the supernatural seem to have become more important in this modern world where spirituality appears to have been traded for technology. From new agers to reborn neo-pagan beliefs, people appear to be embracing a new interest in their quest for the truth about the unknown, much like the Victorian age of spiritualism. Witness popular television and one will be bombarded with programs based on the supernatural and ghosts. And yet, one must ask, why is this so? Do we yearn for something more in our lives, something to suggest that maybe there is life after death? And is it possible that ghosts provide this link? A link to our past?

Over the years I have spoken to many educated, sober, and erudite people from all walks of life. And they have told me stories, some slightly unbelievable, others less so, and yet one thing rings true with all of these reports; so many people tell me that they have witnessed something they cannot explain except to suggest that there is some sort of supernatural element to it. They have no reason to make these tales up, as there is no monetary gain or even fleeting fame. One could say that some of these people are deliberately misleading and one certainly cannot discount this. However, not everyone I speak to could be so wilfully and blatantly lying.

And this leads us to the inevitable conclusion that even if a certain, small percentage of people are making up stories for whatever reason, then we are still left with the sobering fact that there are so many untold reports that simply *cannot* be explained. And if we are to take this further, how is it that so many people over decades, even centuries, and with no connection to each other, continually report seeing the same thing at the same place?

I am often asked whether or not I believe in ghosts. This is a given as I have seen what I consider to be a ghost, not once, but three times. The first being a monk-like figure in a room in the Dragon Inn in Montgomery, Wales; the second, a strange encounter with a small, frail, ghostly woman dressed in brown in the Hellfire Caves in Buckinghamshire, and the third, which was also witnessed by my sister, a fleeting glimpse of a Victorian lady in a white dress who walked past an open door and disappeared. Having said this, I am highly sceptical about a number of reports; after all, how many white ladies, green ladies, and blue ladies can one believe exist? And as such, I have simply presented the stories as I have heard or read them, and so one needs to take it with a grain of salt, even though it has been written in good faith. Ghosts, for whatever reason, seem to integral to all societies over all ages and cultures.

From ruins of ancient Norman structures to the grandeur of restored castles that daily see thousands and thousands of visitors, stories of ghosts abound. And although sceptics may sneer, in these places ghosts are very real. They haunt the ivy-clad ruins of the monasteries and moss-encrusted tombstones of medieval churches. They are the creaks and groans and half-heard whispers in the night and footsteps that scrape upon old wooden staircases. They are the eerie, spine-tingling tapping of fingers on glass and the clanking of chains in neglected dungeons. They are the mysterious hooded figures that haunt our dreams, the headless horsemen who appear out of the cold, swirling mist of the moors.

And with that thought, I shall leave you to your imagination.

BIBLIOGRAPHY

Abrahams, Paul, and Marc Alexander. *In Search of Britain's Haunted Castles*. Stroud, UK: The History Press, 2011.

Arnold, Neil. *Haunted Tunbridge Wells*. Stroud, UK: The History Press, 2013

Arnold, Neil, and Kevin Payne. *Haunted Rochester*. Stroud, UK: The History Press, 2011.

Awford, J. "Is This the Ghost of Anne Boleyn?" *The Daily Mail*. August 2015.

Bloxham, A. "For Sale: King Henry VIII's Haunted Castle." *The Telegraph*. 30 April 2008.

Britton, N. "Hopton Castle, Scene of English Civil War Battle, Saved by Campaigners." *The Telegraph*. 18 November 2008.

Brown, M. "As It Happened: Ghost Hunt at Newcastle's Castle Keep." *The Chronicle*. 23 March 2014.

Burrows, B. "Meet The UK's Scariest Ghosts from Henry VIII's Spirit to Haunting Headless Horsemen." *The Mirror*. 22 April 2014.

Carter, G. "Newark Castle Ghost: Paranormal Investigator 'Captures Haunting Apparition of Fisherwoman.'" *The Mirror*. 7 August 2015.

Cook, T. "Castle Sheds Light on Ghostly Past!" *Harrogate Informer*. 25 October 2013.

Copping, J. "English Heritage Reveals Most Haunted Sites." *The Telegraph*. 27 June 2009.

Crossley, L. "The Castle That Costs Less Than a London Semi." *The Daily Mail* 14 June 2017.

———. "Fancy Being King of the Haunted Castle?" *The Daily Mail*. 10 February 2015.

Dean, J. "Chilling Picture Shows Ghostly Figure in Empty Room at Castle Haunted by Young Girl." *The Mirror*. 7 July 2016.

Evans, S., and Keane D. "Is This Ghostly Figure Hovering in the Ruins of Norfolk Castle the 'She-Wolf of France'?" *The Mirror*. 18 May 2016.

Ferrari, J. "Ghostly Sightings and Spooky Stories from around Huntingdonshire." *Hunts Post*. 25 October 2014.

Fielding, J. "I Survived a Night at Hampton Court Palace with the Ghosts and Ghouls." *The Express*. 29 March 2015.

Fielding, Y., and C. O'Keeffe. *In Search of the Supernatural.* London: Hodder and Stoughton, 2007.

Fields, K. *Lancashire Magic & Mystery: Secrets of the Red Rose County.* Wilmslow, UK: Sigma Press Cheshire 1998.

Fraser, A. "The Hotel In-Spectre! Our Man on a Ghost Hunt in One of Shane Watson's Old Haunts." The *Daily Mail.* 8 August 2013.

Gator, P. *Ghosts at War.* Buxton Derbyshire, UK: Anecdotes, 2009.

Green, Andrew. *Our Haunted Kingdom.* Fontana. 1974.

Halifax, J. "Ghostly Goings on at Dudley Castle." *Birmingham Mail.* 25 June 2015.

Hall, J. "10 Most Haunted Places in Northumberland." *Northumberland Gazette.* 31 October 2015.

Hartland, E. "Somerset's Haunted Locations: 15 of the Scariest Places to Visit." *Somerset Life.* 24 October 2016.

Hynes, K. *Haunted Dartmoor.* Stroud, UK: The History Press, 2014.

Jeeves, P. "Dark Stories from Our Haunted Isle." *Yorkshire Post.* 7 July 2005.

Jones, N. "Houses of Horror: True Sceptic Michaela Strachan Sets Off to Find Britain's Most Haunted House … and Gets Spooked Herself." *Daily Mail.* 11 August 2012.

Joseph, C. "Is This Britain's Most Haunted House?" *Express*. 29 October 2013.

Keegan, S. "Ghost of the Grey Lady Caught on Camera by School Girls at Hampton Court Palace." *The Mirror*. 25 February 2015.

Kirkup, R. *Ghostly County Durham*. Gloucestershire, UK: The History Press. 2010.

Kitchen, R. "Harrogate's Most Haunted." *Harrogate Advertiser*. 31 October 2013.

Knight, D., and C. Hewett. "Ghostly Goings On: Haringey and Enfield's Most Haunted Places." *Enfield Independent*. 19 May 2014.

Kristen, C. *Ghost Trails of Edinburgh and the Borders*. Luton, UK: Andrews UK Limited, 2012.

———. *Ghost Trails of Northumberland and Durham*. Luton, UK: Andrews UK Limited, 2011.

Leadbeater, C., and S. Ryan. "In Search of Henry VIII's Final Queen: Sudeley Castle, and the Sad Story of Katherine Parr." *Daily Mail*. 8 September 2012.

Leatherdale, D. "Raising Spirits." *Northern Echo*. 19 April 2012.

Liddell, Tony. *Supernatural North East: Folklore, Myths, Legends and Ghosts: Otherworld North East Research Society*. Lulu.com, 2009.

Lockley, M. "Dudley Castle Grey Lady Ghost Caught on Camera for First Time." *The Birmingham Mail*. 6 October 2014.

Macrae, F. "Is This Another Ghostly Image Caught on Camera at Britain's Most Haunted Castle?" *Daily Mail*. 2 April 2009.

McKinney, E. "Work Halted on Warwick Castle Over Haunting Scare." *Birmingham Mail*. 16 March 2009.

Montgomery, J. G. *A Case for Ghosts*. Adelaide, Australia: Ginninderra Press, 2012.

———. *Haunted Britain*. Atglen, Pennsylvania: Schiffer Publishing, 2017.

Montgomery, T. "King of the Castle." *Farmers Weekly*. 5 July 2002.

Moore, K. "Tutbury Castle: Is This the Moment Infamous Spook Is Caught on Camera?" *The Mirror*. 7 August 2015.

Morris, J. "Clankety-Clank." *Northern Echo*. 8 January 2014.

Murray, H. "Can You Survive the Night in Cornwall's Most Haunted Castle?" *The Cornishman*. 29 October 2015.

Pasha, M. "The World's Most Haunted Hotels: Old Castles and Former Jails Where Ghosts Roam the Halls." *The Independent*. 1 November 2016.

Pearse, B. *Ghost Hunters Casebook: The Investigations of Andrew Green Revisited*. Stroud, UK: The History Press, 2007.

Polden J. "Is There a Shadow of Doubt?" *Daily Mail*. 7 August 2015.

Richards C. "Caught on Camera: Is This a Ghost Floating Across Entrance to Dover Castle?" *The Mirror*. 15 September 2014.

Ritson, D. *Paranormal County Durham*. Gloucestershire , UK: Amberley Publishing, 2009.

Rodger, J. "Halloween: Scare Yourself Silly at Kenilworth Castle." *The Telegraph*. 21 October 2014.

Romero, K. "Can YOU Spot the Ghost of Henry VIII's Wife in Chilling New Photo?" *The Express*. 30 December 2015.

Saul H. "'Ghost' spotted at Dudley Castle (But are We Just Struggling with a Case of Pareidolia?)." *The Independent*. 8 October 2014.

Sharma S. *Grim History of Newcastle Castle Revealed after £1.67m Restoration*. The *Chronicle*. 21 March 2015.

Simpson J. *It'll Be All Fright on the Night*. The *Telegraph*. 29 October 2005.

Smith O. "London's 11 Most Notorious Public Execution Sites." *The Telegraph*. 18 February 2016 .

Smith, S. "I Saw a Ghost at Corfe Castle." *Daily Echo*. 20 May 2009.

Sophie, A. M. "These Are the 24 Most Haunted Places In Kent." *KentLive*. 28 October 2016.

Spencer, A. *The Tale Of The Wronged Lady*. BBC Home. February 2005.

Stanley, T. Ghost hunt: "'The Crypt Was Large and Empty. Then I Realised I Was Not Alone.'" *The Telegraph*. 27 March 2014.

Underwood, P. *Ghosts of Kent: Authentic Ghost Stories From The Garden Of England*. Sittingbourne, UK: Meresborough Books, 1984.

———. *Haunted Farnham*. Stroud, UK: The History Press, 2013.

———. *Where the Ghosts Walk: The Gazetteer of Haunted Britain*. London: Souvenir Press, 2013.

Westwood, J., and J. Simpson. *Haunted England: The Penguin Book of Ghosts*. London: Penguin, 2010.

White, G., ed. *Ghost Stories from the North of England*. 2013.

Wilkes, D. "Chilling Image of 'Grey Lady Ghost' Captured in Archway." *Daily Mail*. 7 October 2014.

Winchester, L. "Is This Anne Boleyn?" *The Express*. 3 August 2015.

Worsley, L. "Eek! There Are Ghosts in My Royal Palace." *Daily Mail*. 7 March 2015.

WEBLINKS

www.ghost-story.co.uk

www.thetudorbookblog.com

www.visitkent.co.uk

www.nationaltrust.org.uk

www.haunted-britain.com

www.legendarydartmoor.co.uk

www.yha.org.uk

www.haunted-britain.com

www.hauntedrooms.co.uk

www.ournottinghamshire.org.uk

www.mysteriousbritain.co.uk

www.britainirelandcastles.com

www.espncricinfo.com

www.castlesandmanorhouses.com

www.bbc.co.uk

www.thisisdurham.com

www.english-heritage.org.uk

www.worldofghosts.co.uk

www.english-heritage.org.uk

www.nottinghamcastle.org.uk

www.haunted-yorkshire.co.uk

www.english-heritage.org.uk

www.britainexpress.com

www.davidfarrant.org

www.paranormaldatabase.com

www.english-heritage.org.uk

www.ghostsofthenortheast.co.uk

www.paranormaltours.com

www.on-magazine.co.uk/yorkshire

www.devonhampers.com

www.hauntedrooms.co.uk

www.ghost-story.co.uk

www.castleofspirits.com

www.haunted-yorkshire.co.uk

www.hauntedhovel.com

http://hampshireghostclub.net

http://shropshirehistory.com

https://hauntedhistoryoflincolnshire.blogs.lincoln.ac.uk

http://hauntedwiltshire.blogspot.com.au

http://onthetudortrail.com

https://museumofsomerset.org.uk

https://great-castles.com

CASTLE WEBSITES

www.hrp.org.uk/tower-of-london

www.haringey.gov.uk/bruce-castle-museum

www.amberleycastle.co.uk

www.hrp.org.uk/hampton-court-palace

www.arundelcastle.org

www.dorkingmuseum.org.uk/local-history/great-estates
/betchworth-castle

www.nationaltrust.org.uk/bodiam-castle

www.english-heritage.org.uk/visit/places
/donnington-castle

www.english-heritage.org.uk/visit/places/dover-castle

www.farnhamcastle.com

www.discoverhastings.co.uk

www.herstmonceux-castle.com

www.hevercastle.co.uk

www.leeds-castle.com

www.oxfordcastleunlocked.co.uk

www.english-heritage.org.uk/visit/places/pevensey-castle

www.english-heritage.org.uk/visit/places
/portchester-castle

www.english-heritage.org.uk/visit/places/rochester-castle

www.nationaltrust.org.uk/sissinghurst-castle

www.royalcollection.org.uk/visit/windsorcastle

www.berkeley-castle.com

www.english-heritage.org.uk/visit/places
/berry-pomeroy-castle

www.nationaltrust.org.uk/corfe-castle

www.nationaltrust.org.uk/dunster-castle

www.english-heritage.org.uk/visit/places
/farleigh-hungerford-castle

www.english-heritage.org.uk/visit/places
/lydford-castle-and-saxon-town

https://museumofsomerset.org.uk/taunton-castle

www.english-heritage.org.uk/visit/places
/okehampton-castle

www.english-heritage.org.uk/visit/places
/old-wardour-castle

www.english-heritage.org.uk/visit/places/pendennis-castle

www.pengersickcastle.com

www.powderham.co.uk

www.english-heritage.org.uk/visit/places/st-briavels-castle

www.sudeleycastle.co.uk

www.tivertoncastle.com

www.english-heritage.org.uk/visit/places
/baconsthorpe-castle

www.english-heritage.org.uk/visit/places
/castle-rising-castle

https://cimuseums.org.uk/visit/venues/colchester-castle

www.english-heritage.org.uk/visit/places
/framlingham-castle

www.english-heritage.org.uk/visit/places/hadleigh-castle

www.kimbolton.cambs.sch.uk/castle

www.museums.norfolk.gov.uk/Visit_Us/Norwich_Castle

www.gatehouse-gazetteer.info/English%20sites/2994.html

www.castleuk.net/castle_lists_midlands/141
/barnwellcastle.htm

www.english-heritage.org.uk/visit/places/bolsover-castle

www.lincolncastle.com

www.newark-sherwooddc.gov.uk/newarkcastle

www.nottinghamcastle.org.uk

www.english-heritage.org.uk/visit/places/peveril-castle

www.nationaltrust.org.uk/tattershall-castle

www.english-heritage.org.uk/visit/places
/acton-burnell-castle

www.arburyestate.co.uk/index.php?page=astley-castle

www.dudleyzoo.org.uk/dudley-castle

www.english-heritage.org.uk/visit/places/goodrich-castle

www.hoptoncastle.org.uk

www.english-heritage.org.uk/visit/places/kenilworth-castle

www.ludlowcastle.com

www.tamworthcastle.co.uk

www.tutburycastle.com

www.warwick-castle.com

www.whittingtoncastle.co.uk

http://askertoncastle.co.uk/history

www.english-heritage.org.uk/visit/places/carlisle-castle

www.visitcumbria.com/pen/dacre-castle

http://leasowecastle.com

www.lowthercastle.org

www.muncaster.co.uk

www.naworth.co.uk

www.visitcumbria.com/evnp/pendragon-castle

www.boltoncastle.co.uk

www.english-heritage.org.uk/visit/places
    /conisbrough-castle

www.english-heritage.org.uk/visit/places/helmsley-castle

www.harrogate.gov.uk/info/20153
    /knaresborough_castle_and_museum

www.english-heritage.org.uk/visit/places
    /middleham-castle

www.english-heritage.org.uk/visit/places/pickering-castle

www.pontefractcastle.co.uk

www.english-heritage.org.uk/visit/places/richmond-castle

www.ripleycastle.co.uk

www.english-heritage.org.uk/visit/places
    /scarborough-castle

www.castlesfortsbattles.co.uk/yorkshire/sheriff_hutton
_castle.html

www.skiptoncastle.co.uk

www.english-heritage.org.uk/visit/places/spofforth-castle

www.bamburghcastle.com

www.english-heritage.org.uk/visit/places/barnard-castle

www.heartofhadrianswall.com
/forts-and-castles/82-bellister-castle

www.english-heritage.org.uk/visit/places/bowes-castle

www.blenkinsoppcastleinn.co.uk

www.newcastlecastle.co.uk

www.chillingham-castle.com

www.english-heritage.org.uk/visit/places
/dunstanburgh-castle

www.durhamworldheritagesite.com/architecture/castle

www.heartofhadrianswall.com
/forts-and-castles/83-featherstone-castle

www.haughtoncastle.com

www.nationaltrust.org.uk/lindisfarne-castle

www.english-heritage.org.uk/visit/places/prudhoe-castle

www.rabycastle.com

www.celticcastles.com/castles/walworth-castle

www.english-heritage.org.uk/visit/places
/warkworth-castle-and-hermitage

ABOUT THE AUTHOR

J. G. Montgomery is a forty-something-year-old public servant. He was born in Cornwall in the United Kingdom, the son of an Australian Air Force officer. He is a bass player, guitarist, vocalist, and song writer in a mod rock band and has served in both the Australian Army Reserve and Australian Air Force. He has university degrees in cultural heritage and teaching and was once a cricket coach. He is also a decorated State Emergency Service volunteer. DNA testing on his mother's side suggests that he is related to Queen Victoria as well as Richard III.

Haunted Castles of England is his eighth book. He is also the author of *A Case for Ghosts* (Ginninderra Press, 2012), the illustrated children's book *The Oomee Mau Mau* (Willow Moon, 2012), *WYRD: A Journey into the Beliefs and Philosophies of the Known and Unknown* (CFZ Press, 2014), *Meditations in Orange* (Pendragon Publishing & Design, 2014), *Summer to Summer* (Pendragon Publishing & Design, 2017), *Haunted Britain: Supernatural Realms of the United Kingdom* (Schiffer Publishing, 2017) and *Haunted Australia: Ghosts of the Great Southern Land* (Schiffer Publishing, 2017).

He also contributed and edited poetry in *Capital Reflections* (Pendragon Publishing & Design, 2014) and has written screenplays for a number of short documentaries.

He lives in Canberra, Australia, with his partner, Kirsten, three cats, a short black dog, six ducks, and a lot of goldfish.